The Kogan Page Market Research Series breaks new ground in market research publishing. While most books tend to be all-embracing tomes covering every aspect of market research, each title in this new series is devoted to a specific technique or key area.

The prime aim of the titles in the series is to demystify the technicalities of market research by providing concise, digestible introductions, presented in a clear and comprehensive style.

Well illustrated throughout, these practical guides will serve as vital introductions for those new to market research, useful revision tools for students and essential refreshers for all market research professionals.

Titles in the series are:

> *Questionnaire Design*
> *Interviewing*
> *Sampling and Statistics*
> *Desk Research*
> *Presentations and Report Writing*
> *Buying Market Research*

D0583058

ABOUT THE AUTHOR

■

Paul Hague is a Chairman of Business and Market Research PLC. He regularly contributes to the market research trade press and lectures at seminars on the subject. He is author of *The Industrial Market Research Handbook* and co-author of *Do Your Own Market Research, How to do Marketing Research* and *Market Research in Practice*. He is also joint editor of *A Handbook of Market Research Techniques*. All these books are published by Kogan Page.

QUESTIONNAIRE DESIGN

Paul Hague

KOGAN
PAGE

001. 43HAG
157754 research
skills
7 day

LRC Stoke Park
GUILDFORD COLLEGE

First published in 1993
Reprinted 1994
Reprinted 1998

Apart from any fair dealing for the purposes of research or private study, or criticism or review, as permitted under the Copyright, Designs and Patents Act, 1988, this publication may only be reproduced, stored or transmitted, in any form or by any means, with the perior permission in writing of the publishers, or in the case of reprographic reproduction in accordance with the terms of licences issued by the Copyright Licensing Agency. Enquiries concerning reproduction outside those terms should be sent to the publishers at the undermentioned address:

Kogan Page Limited
120 Pentonville Road
London N1 9JN

© Paul Hague, 1993

British Library Cataloguing in Publication Data

A CIP record for this book is available from the British Library.

ISBN 0 7494 0917 7

Typeset by BookEns Limited, Royston, Herts.
Printed in England by Clays Ltd, St Ives plc

CONTENTS

■

PREFACE

■

This book is part of a series which focuses on specific subjects in the market researcher's armoury including questionnaire design, interviewing, sampling and reporting.

There are dozens of books available on market research and, in part, I have been responsible for a number of them. However, hardly any of them cover the fundamental subject of questionnaire design. Some years ago I read an excellent book* by William Belson which takes apart a tried and tested questionnaire used in a readership survey. It was frightening to see how even the simplest of questions can be misconstrued. Gradually my confidence returned and I realised that questionnaire design is a skill, guided by rules and principles, but it is also an art and as such is influenced by flair.

Perhaps there is good reason why there are so few books on questionnaire design — it is a subject on which an author is laid wide open to criticism. Every word in a question can be put under scrutiny. The order of the words in each question, nay, the order and style of the questions themselves, are all open to debate. The examples of questions in this book, which purports to be a guide to good questionnaire design, should be honed to perfection and yet I fear exposure since everyone is open to misinterpretation by somebody.

---

*William Belson, *Design And Understanding Of Survey Questions*, 1982, Gower Press, Aldershot.

However, all is not lost. Good questionnaires are workable questionnaires. They are questionnaires which elicit the truth. The perfect questionnaire has never been designed. Give a room full of researchers a market research task to solve and, even if the research method is the same (and the chances are there will be some marked variations), the questionnaires which drive the interviews will be different. This diversity of approaches is not wrong, it simply points to the flexibility of the questioning process which leads to the truth.

The market research industry is staffed with people who have studied a multiplicity of disciplines. Many are young, enthusiastic and inexperienced in business. Nevertheless they are researchers and must do their best in the search for the truth. Very often they are thrown in the deep end and asked to 'knock up a questionnaire and find something out about this, that or the other'. They learn their craft by looking over other people's shoulders. Tips are picked up from other questionnaires and the researcher's own effort is then screened, first by an experienced colleague and ultimately in the field where it is tried and tested as a working tool.

In theory it is in the field that a questionnaire lives or dies. However, such is the skill of most interviewers, that even the most crass of questionnaires can be made to work in their hands. Answers to poor questions are achieved and the researcher could be deluded for long enough into thinking that his or her questionnaire design skills have been perfected. Certainly, over time they will improve as experience is the key to all market research tasks. But experience is another word for learning from mistakes and this can be costly, since the *raison d'être* of market research is to reduce business risk. Learning the craft at someone else's expense is a dangerous game to play.

It is hoped that this book will be received in good spirit. It is a practitioner's guide to designing questionnaires with lots of encouragement to 'have a go' because practice makes perfect. It contains numerous examples to stimulate and to give ideas. Look critically at the book. Look critically at your own and other people's questionnaires. When questions are found to work, remember which they are and use them again and again. Keep a file of questionnaires to look at. Most of all, listen to the criticism that the interviewers level against them since they are the people who know what really does work.

Paul Hague
March 1993

1

THE ROLE OF QUESTIONNAIRES

■

Questionnaire design is one of the basic building blocks of market research. Indeed, think of a market researcher and you may think of someone, clipboard in hand, asking questions and writing the answers on a questionnaire. However, the questionnaire is not an end in itself: it is a vehicle by which people are interviewed. A questionnaire provides the interviewer with a form on which to record answers; without it the interview has no structure. Data processing departments use the completed questionnaire to produce an analysis of the response.

The questionnaire does not, therefore, stand in isolation; it is an aid to the collection of data in an interview. At the same time as thinking about designing the questionnaire, the researcher should keep in mind the wider context in which the questionnaire will be used. How many interviews will there be? Who will be interviewed? How will the interview be carried out? Who will be administering the interview? Cognisance of these broader issues will help the researcher design questionnaires which work.

THE FOUR PURPOSES OF QUESTIONNAIRES

The questionnaire fulfils four purposes:

■   Primarily the role of a questionnaire is to draw accurate information from the respondent. The researcher is trying to obtain as close a picture as is possible of what is happening in the marketplace. Accurate information is obtained by asking the right question of the right person.

■ The questionnaire provides a structure to the interview so that it flows smoothly and orderly. It is important in any survey of more than just a few people that all respondents are asked the same questions in exactly the same way. Without this structure there would be chaos and it would be impossible to build the overall picture. The questionnaire acts as an *aide-mémoire* for the interviewer preventing an 'anything goes' situation. For the respondent it gives a logical sequence to the questions, driving towards a point and moving smoothly on to the next subject.

■ The third purpose of the questionnaire is to provide a standard format on which facts, comments and attitudes can be recorded. A record of an interview is essential, otherwise points could be forgotten or distorted. Of course, a paper questionnaire is not the only means by which the information is recorded; a tape recorder is an excellent means of capturing data. However, tapes have their disadvantages. They can break down and they run out. In certain circumstances they may inhibit the response. They are also time consuming to listen to and interpret after the event. Besides, even when a tape is used, a questionnaire is also needed to *guide* the discussion.

■ Finally, the questionnaire facilitates data processing. The various answers are recorded in a place where the data processing team know where to find them. Without a questionnaire a survey of 500 people would produce 500 jottings or free-ranging interviews which are burdensome to process.

Throughout the book examples are used to illustrate the various points. However, at this early stage it may be helpful for the reader to view a questionnaire in its entirety in order to obtain a feel for the subject. The following sample questionnaire was administered by telephone and the interview took between 15 and 20 minutes to complete.

ALUMINIUM WINDOW SURVEY

Company Name: ....

Address: ....

....

....

Respondent Name & Position: ....

Fieldworker: ....

Date: ....

Good morning/afternoon. This is ..... from Business & Market Research in Manchester. I am carrying out a survey into trends in the aluminium window market and I wonder if you could help me. It will only take about fifteen minutes. Before I start can I make sure that you fabricate domestic aluminium windows or doors? (ONLY INTERVIEW COMPANIES THAT DO SO).

Q1.   First of all, can I check if you fabricate any other types of domestic replacement windows or doors?

UPVC	1
Softwood	2
Hardwood	3
Steel	4
Only aluminium	5
Others (SPECIFY)	6

....

Roughly, what proportion of your domestic window or door business, in value terms is in ...... (SPECIFY THE DIFFERENT MATERIALS FROM WHICH THE FABRICATORS MAKES WINDOWS)?

		<5%	6-20%	21-40%	41-60%	61-85%	86-99%	100%	None
Q2a	Aluminium?	1	2	3	4	5	6	7	8
Q2b	UPVC?	1	2	3	4	5	6	7	8
Q2c	Softwood?	1	2	3	4	5	6	7	8
Q2d	Hardwood?	1	2	3	4	5	6	7	8
Q2e	Steel?	1	2	3	4	5	6	7	8
Q2f	Other?	1	2	3	4	5	6	7	8

Q3a.   What particular advantages does a domestic aluminium range offer you? (DO NOT PROMPT)

Meets customer demand	1
Offers an alternative	2
Looks better in certain houses	3
Stronger/more durable	4
Easier to fabricate	5
Cheaper/better value than UPVC	6
Wider range of finish/colours	7
Low maintenance	8
Good insulation properties	9
Condensation free	10
Other (SPECIFY)	11
....	12

(ASK ONLY IF UPVC WINDOWS ARE FABRICATED)
Q3b.   What particular advantages does a UPVC domestic range offer you?
(DO NOT PROMPT)

Meets customer demand	1
Offers an alternative	2
Looks better in certain houses	3
Stronger/more durable	4
Easier to fabricate	5
Cheaper/better value than UPVC	6
Wider range of finish/colours	7
Low maintenance	8
Good insulation properties	9
Condensation free	10
Other (SPECIFY)	11
....	12

Q4a.   Looking to the future, would you expect your sales of aluminium windows or doors for the domestic
market, to increase, decrease or stay the same over the next three years?

Increase	1	**Q4b**
Stay the same/don't know	2	**Q4d**
Decrease	3	**Q4d**
Refused	4	**Q4f**

Q4b.   Why do you think that your sales of domestic aluminium windows will increase over the next three
years? (DO NOT PROMPT)

Market buoyant/increasing	1
Innovations in aluminium design	2
Aluminium more competitive	3
UPVC degenerates over time	4
Aluminium easier to work with	5
Aluminium more profitable for me	6
Will push aluminium more in future	7
Other (SPECIFY)	8
....	9

Q4c.   Can I ask you to imagine that your sales of domestic aluminium windows and doors are 100 at the present, what do you think they could be in three years time, in 1996?

100	1
101 - 105	2
106 - 110	3
111 - 120	4
121 - 140	5
141 - 150	6
151 - 180	7
Over 180	8
Don't know	9

Q4d.   Why do you think that your sales of aluminium windows and doors will stay the same/decline over the next three years?

UPVC will steal sales	1
Hardwood will steal sales	2
Competition fierce in aluminium	3
Fall in demand for replacement windows	4
Not a profitable market	5
Will get out of aluminium in future	6
Other (SPECIFY)	7
....	8

Q4e.   Can I ask you to imagine that your sales of domestic aluminium windows or doors are 100 at the present, what do you think they could be in three years time in 1996?

100	1
90 - 99	2
80 - 89	3
60 - 79	4
50 - 59	5
Will get out of aluminium by then	6
Don't know	7

ASK ALL

Q4f.   What changes do you foresee within the market for different types of domestic aluminium systems? **PROBE:** What about thermal brakes? What about different colours? What about finishes? What about doors as opposed to windows - which do you think will grow faster?

....

....

Q5a.   Could I now ask you which manufacturers you are aware of that supply domestic aluminium systems to companies such as yourself? **PROBE:** Any others? **DO NOT PROMPT.**

Q5b.   I am now going to read out some other companies that supply this market. As I read them out, would you tell me which you have heard of? READ OUT ONLY THOSE NOT RINGED AT Q5a. ROTATE THE ORDER PLEASE.

	Q5a	Q5b
Adeptal	1	1
Alcan	2	2
AWS	3	3
Cego Crittall	4	4
Coastal	5	5
Consort	6	6
Duraflex	7	7
Glostal	8	8
HIS	9	9
Monarch	10	10
Prime	11	11
Scope	12	12
Schuco	13	13
Smart Systems	14	14
Other (SPECIFY)	15	15
	16	16

Now could I check out your views on some of these system companies that you are aware of. Which do you think is best in the domestic aluminium market for. . .?

Q6a.   delivery?

Q6b.   price?

Q6c.   quality?

	Q6a	Q6b	Q6c
Adeptal	1	1	1
Alcan	2	2	2
AWS	3	3	3
Cego Crittall	4	4	4
Coastal	5	5	5
Consort	6	6	6
Duraflex	7	7	7
Glostal	8	8	8
HIS	9	9	9
Monarch	10	10	10
Prime	11	11	11
Scope	12	12	12
Schuco	13	13	13
Smart Systems	14	14	14
Other (SPECIFY)	15	15	15
	16	16	16

Q7a. And now finally in this series of questions on companies, can I ask you which companies you use yourselves as suppliers of domestic aluminium systems?

Adeptal	1
Alcan	2
AWS	3
Cego Crittall	4
Coastal	5
Consort	6
Duraflex	7
Glostal	8
HIS	9
Monarch	10
Prime	11
Scope	12
Schuco	13
Smart Systems	14
Other (SPECIFY)	15
....	16

Q7b. Are there any other companies supplying domestic aluminium systems that you would not use?

Yes	1	**Q7c**
No	2	**Q8a**

Q7c. Which companies are they?

Adeptal	1
Alcan	2
AWS	3
Cego Crittall	4
Coastal	5
Consort	6
Duraflex	7
Glostal	8
HIS	9
Monarch	10
Prime	11
Scope	12
Schuco	13
Smart Systems	14
Other (SPECIFY)	15
....	16

Q7d. Why wouldn't you use this company? (STATE COMPANY IF RESPONDENT WOULDN'T USE MORE THAN ONE)?

....

....

Q8a. What above all else do you look for when choosing an aluminium system supplier for domestic window or door frames? PROMPT & ROTATE FACTORS.

Wide range of aluminium systems	1
Rapid delivery	2
Assured delivery	3
Competitive prices	4
Technical advice	5
Good sales service	6
High quality systems	7
(Don't know)	8

Q8b. Is there anything else important?

Yes	1	**Q8c**
No	2	**Q9a**

Q8c. What else is important?

. . . .

. . . .

Q9a. I am on the last leg now and you have been most patient. My final questions are simply to classify the information you have just given me. As with all the data it will be treated as absolutely confidential to ourselves. Which of the following activities are you involved in for the domestic market? READ OUT LIST

Aluminium windows	1
Aluminium doors	2
UPVC windows	3
UPVC doors	4
Other windows	5
Other doors	6
(Refused)	7

Q9b. Are there any other important sides to your business outside of these I have just mentioned?

Yes	1	**Q9c**
No	2	**Q10a**

Q9c. What else do you do?

. . . .

. . . .

Very roughly, what proportion of your business in aluminium windows and doors is. . . .

		<5%	5-30%	31-80%	81-99%	100%	DK/not stated	None
Q10a	domestic?	1	2	3	4	5	6	7
Q10b	commercial or industrial?	1	2	3	4	5	6	7

Q11.   What were your total purchases of aluminium section used for domestic replacement windows and doors in 1993? Please exclude any section that may be used to reinforce UPVC windows or doors. RECORD ANSWER IN EITHER £ OR TONNES BELOW.

Under £25k (33 tonnes)	1
£26k - £200k (34 - 267 tonnes)	2
£201k - £750k (268 - 1,000 tonnes)	3
£751k - £1,500k (1,001 - 2,000 tonnes)	4
£1,501 - £2,500 (2,001 - 3,333 tonnes)	5
Over £2,500k (3,334 + tonnes)	6
Don't know/won't say/refused	7

Q12.   LOCATION

North	1
Midlands	2
South	3

THANK & CLOSE

2

DECIDING WHAT TYPE OF QUESTIONNAIRE TO USE

■

Researchers recognise three different types of interview situations which in turn require three different types of questionnaires:

1. *Structured.* In structured interviews, the questionnaires set out precisely the wording of the questions and the order in which they will be asked. Most of the questions have predefined answers and there will be little latitude for a respondent to stray beyond them. Structured questionnaires and interviews are the bedrock of large quantitative surveys.

2. *Semi-structured.* This type of interview uses questionnaires with a mixture of questions with predefined answers as well as those where the respondent is free to say whatever is liked. In each interview the questions are asked in the same way and there may be hundreds of interviews in the whole survey. The semi-structured questionnaire is a more flexible tool than its highly structured counterpart and there is likely to be more probing to find out the reasons for certain answers.

3. *Unstructured.* In this type of informal, or *depth* interview, the researcher uses a checklist of questions rather than a

formal questionnaire on which the answers are written down. There is considerable latitude allowed on the part of the interviewer and different channels of questioning will be selected during the interview itself. The interview is very often recorded on tape.

Whether the researcher uses a structured, semi-structured or unstructured questionnaire depends on the number of people who will be interviewed, what type of people they are, the type of information which is being collected and the type of interviewers who will be administering the questions. The method of data analysis also has an influence, though in itself this is influenced by the size of the survey and the type of information collected.

AN EXAMPLE OF A SURVEY USING STRUCTURED INTERVIEWS

A company manufacturing bread wants to test consumer awareness of different brands of bread and to collect data on the types of bread people are buying. The company sells in a tight geographical area which is approximately defined by a radius of 100 miles from the bakery. This encompasses four major cities and numerous small towns, a total population of approximately five million. A decision is made to collect the data in street interviews, targeting women over the age of 18 and ensuring that the interviewers do not stand within 100 yards of a shop which sells bread. A total of 2000 interviews are to be carried out from 20 sampling points, these to be chosen randomly from the towns and cities which are divided into 200 squares by a grid overlaying a map of the area.

The critical factors which influence the type of questionnaire used to collect information for the bakery are:

- street interviews. This means the interview needs to be short, say around 10 or 15 minutes at the most.
- female respondents. In the main, the respondents will have a predictable buying pattern for bread.
- 2000 interviews. With this large number, questions should

be pre-coded to aid data processing and to make the interviewing task itself easier.
■ a fieldforce of interviewers spread around the territory, one at each interviewing point, and in the main working without supervision.

The type of questionnaire that is used in this survey will need to be *structured*, allowing the interviewer little room for manoeuvre beyond the way the questions are laid down.

AN EXAMPLE OF A SURVEY USING SEMI-STRUCTURED INTERVIEWS

A company makes central heating boilers which it sells through distributors to plumbers or heating and ventilating engineers who carry out the installation. The central heating boilers are fitted in new property, or go into older property to replace boilers which are past their useful life. Sometimes the boilers are installed in property which has never enjoyed the luxury of central heating. The company wants to find out where it is positioned in this market against the multiplicity of domestic and foreign suppliers and is seeking some insights into how it can build its market share. A research programme is devised based on 500 interviews with installers throughout the country. The interviews will be carried out by telephone as this is thought to be the best way of getting hold of a random sample of busy installers. It is estimated that each interview will take around 20 minutes.

The forces which influence the type of questionnaire which should be used in this survey are:

■ telephone interviews. This medium requires a relatively simple questionnaire which can be completed in 20 minutes.
■ an interviewer force working by telephone from a central location. This gives the facility to control and support the interviewers as the work is progressing and it allows interviewers to share problems to their mutual benefit.
■ respondents who are installers. These people are likely to represent companies which are variable in size and interests

from the 'one-man-band' plumber to heating and ventilating engineers who could employ hundreds of people. The range of responses from these different people will be hard to pre-empt.

■ 500 interviews. This is a sufficiently large number to require a questionnaire designed to overcome analysis problems.

This study will need to have built-in flexibility to accommodate the range of replies from the different groups of respondents. Questions which aim to find out about buying motivations would be difficult to pre-code as they could vary considerably according to the size of installer, the number of installations that he carries out and the type of customer for whom the installer is working.

Open-ended questions will almost certainly be necessary and the interviewers will have to be well briefed to ensure that they can probe in depth and offer explanations should respondents face difficulties in providing answers. (An open-ended question is one where the respondent is free to give any answer and this is written down verbatim. Such questions are useful for teasing out the subtleties that may not surface in a closed question. More about open and closed questions in Chapter 3).

The questionnaire which will be used in the boiler survey will contain a mixture of closed and open-ended questions and will, therefore, be *semi-structured*.

AN EXAMPLE OF A SURVEY USING UNSTRUCTURED INTERVIEWS

A third company sells pension plans to private individuals, many of them self-employed. This is a fiercely competitive market in which the target customers need a great deal of persuasion to invest in a pension at all and, furthermore, they are ignorant of the schemes and distrustful of the people who sell them. The company selling the pension plans has asked its advertising agency to devise a new and innovative campaign which will differentiate the company and draw enquiries for its salesforce to chase. The researchers decided upon a qualitative approach, screening out self-employed people aged 30 to 40 years, who are currently without a pension and with the objective of carrying out 30 face-to-face interviews in total.

This survey needs to find out how potential investors learn about pension products and how they could be imaginatively advertised. The survey is concerned with understanding the feelings people have towards pension companies and the triggers and barriers which, on the one hand, prompt an enquiry, and on the other hand which limit interest. Such insights are best obtained by depth interviewing and the factors which will influence the type of questionnaire (or in this case checklist) which should be used are:

- interviews will be in-depth and one-to-one. In the interviews respondents will be encouraged to open up beyond the obvious answers such as 'all pension companies are the same', 'it is a long way off my pension and I have far better things to do with my money'.
- only two interviewers will be used so that they are able to build up knowledge of the subject and improve the incisiveness of their questions. The interviewers will be senior people on the team, experts in qualitative research.
- respondents will be self-made people or those who aspire to be self-made. They will be people who are short on time and patience and who are prima donnas in that they are driven to succeed.
- 30 interviews is the size of the sample. This is a small enough number to be able to treat each respondent as a case history and to develop specific questions pertinent to a particular respondent. Equally, the researchers will be looking for some patterns of response as the aim is to find common triggers and messages for an advertising campaign. The two researchers must, therefore, work from the same list of questions.

This type of questioning needs to be adaptable and stimulating. It must encourage respondents to open the lids of their minds and give the researchers the facility to probe and follow interesting paths of discussion. The questions will be listed as subjects to cover and will be referred to now and then by the interviewer during the interview to ensure that all the topics have been covered. The precise wording of the questions will be crafted during the interview itself and almost certainly, additional ones will be added when appropriate. In essence, the interview and the questionnaire will be *unstructured*.

A CLASSIFICATION OF QUESTIONNAIRES

Clearly these three research scenarios do not represent the whole cross-section of possibilities but they illustrate the different types of interviews and questionnaires which researchers can use.

The three different classifications are summarised below:

TABLE 2.I A CLASSIFICATION OF QUESTIONNAIRES

Type of questionnaire	Areas of use of questionnaire	Administration of the questionnaire
Structured	Used in large interview programmes (anything over 50 interviews). Typically used where it is possible to closely anticipate the possible responses.	Telephone/ Face-to-face/ Self completion
Semi-structured	Used widely in business-to-business market research where there is a need to accommodate different responses from companies. Also used where the responses cannot be anticipated.	Face-to-face/ Telephone

Type of questionnaire	Areas of use of questionnaire	Administration of the questionnaire
Unstructured	The basis of many studies into technical or narrow markets. Also used in depth interviewing and in group discussions. Allows probing and searching where a skilled researcher is not fully sure of the responses before the interview.	Group discussions/ Industrial visit interviews/ Depth telephone interviews

THREE DIFFERENT TYPES OF QUESTIONS

■

Structured and semi-structured questionnaires are made up of three different types of questions depending on the type of information which is being collected.

TABLE 3.I A CLASSIFICATION OF QUESTIONS

Type of question	Information sought	Types of surveys where used
Behavioural	Factual information on what the respondent is, does or owns. Also the frequency with which certain actions are carried out. Where people live.	Surveys to find out market size, market shares, awareness, usage rates.
Attitudinal	What people think of something. Their image and ratings of things. Why they do things.	Image and attitude surveys. Brand mapping studies. Surveys to help build market share.

Type of question	Information sought	Types of surveys where used
Classification	Information that can be used to group respondents to see how they differ one from the other — such as age, gender, social class, location of household, type of house, family composition.	All surveys.

BEHAVIOURAL QUESTIONS

Behavioural questions seek to find out what people (or companies) do. For example, do people go to the cinema, how often do they go, what type of cinema do they visit, who do they go with etc? They determine people's actions in terms of what they have eaten (or drunk), bought, used, visited, seen, read or heard. Behavioural questions record *facts* and not matters of opinion.

Behavioural questions address the following:

- Have you ever . . . ?
- Do you ever . . . ?
- Who do you know . . . ?
- When did you last . . . ?
- Which do you do most often . . . ?
- Who does it . . . ?
- How many . . . ?
- Do you have . . . ?
- In what way do you do it . . . ?
- In the future will you . . . ?

ATTITUDINAL QUESTIONS

Attitudes are opinions or basic beliefs which people have about the products they buy and the companies they deal with, and it is attitudes that motivate people in their actions. Attitudes towards a subject could be misguided and wrong, but this is hardly relevant since it is *perceptions* which count. The attitudes which people have will guide the way they act.

The way people react to situations depends on their attitudes and so they can be deemed to be favourable or unfavourable. Researchers need to measure these to find out what disposition is held and how it could affect the buying decision.

Matters of opinion are collected by attitudinal questions. As the term suggests, these questions seek to uncover people's beliefs and thoughts on a subject.

Attitudinal questions address the following:

■   What do you think of . . . ?
■   Why do you . . . ?
■   Do you agree or disagree . . . ?
■   How do you rate . . . ?
■   Which is best (or worst) for . . . ?

Attitudes or opinions are always important in surveys as they are pointers towards people's motivations and therefore their likely buying habits. However, whereas answers to behavioural questions can be assumed to be correct (unless someone is deliberately lying or the question is stretching the bounds of their ability to answer), answers to attitudinal questions may need considerable interpretation.

Take for example a question which seeks to find out the likelihood of buying a new product. The respondents may be asked to sample the product and state whether or not they would buy it. To gauge the likelihood of buying the product, responses could be collected on a five point scale running from very likely through to very unlikely, ie:

> Very likely
> Quite likely
> Neither likely nor unlikely
> Quite unlikely
> Very unlikely

Assuming that 20 per cent of the people interviewed said that they were very likely to buy the product and 30 per cent said that they were quite likely to buy it, what would the true proportions be that would make the purchase? The chances are that when people have to part with money to buy the product, the proportions will fall dramatically. It would not be surprising to find that only half the people who showed some disposition to buying the product at the time of the interview (saying they were very or quite likely) would actually do so. Thus, unlike behavioural questions which collect factual information, attitudinal questions need interpretation to make sense.

On the other hand, there are circumstances when conditioning and advertising leads to an increase in the disposition to buy with the result that the proportions who said that they were likely to buy the product at the time of the interview are grossly understated.

One of the best means of assessing the relevance and meaning of attitudinal questions is by reference to benchmarks. By way of example, respondents taking part in a customer satisfaction survey may be asked to rate a company on a scale. For example:

> And now I would like you to tell me what you think of a couple of suppliers of XXX (a product) which you know. I would like you to give me a score out of 5 where 5 is very good and 1 is very poor. (SCORE 6 FOR DON'T KNOW, WON'T SAY) Can I start with . . . ? (NAME THE COMPANY) What do you think of this company for . . . ?

What does it mean if a company achieves an average score of 3.7 for the quality of its products and 4.2 for its deliveries? The researcher would interpret the results, comparing the scores of one company with another, but also using the 'normative' data built up over many similar surveys almost certainly in a variety of markets. Thus, besides saying where a company stands one to another, experience from many other surveys may enable the researcher to say that:

4.0 to 5.0	is a score which may be expected by a market leader;
3.5 to 3.9	is a score which is acceptable but needs improvement;
3.0 to 3.4	is a score which is bordering on the acceptable but needs considerable improvement;
<3.0	is a score which in most customer surveys would be deemed unacceptable.

These interpretations are typical of the problems faced by researchers who have to unravel the answers to attitudinal questions.

Attitudinal questions must be couched in a manner that is meaningful to respondents. This could determine the language used in the question, whether it is asked using words in a scale (a verbal rating scale), numbers (a numerical rating scale) or a list of statements where the respondent is asked to agree or disagree or rank them in order. Examples of scalar questions are given in Chapter 5.

Deciding on the terminology for attitudinal questions could well involve some depth interviewing before the questionnaire is designed. For example, imagine a study which aims to collect people's attitudes to cars. What question could be asked to determine the level of interest held in cars? With the benefit of earlier depth research, the researcher may have learned that a barometer of interest is to ask people how much they like talking about cars. Thus, a question which could be used to classify or segment people, and using terminology which is relevant to the subject, could be:

Q   On a scale from 1 to 5, would you say that you like talking about cars a lot or a little? A score of 5 means you like talking about cars a lot and a score of 1 means you like talking about cars a little.

This seems obvious when it is pointed out but it need not necessarily occur to the researcher at the time of designing the questionnaire and without the benefit of qualitative research.

Think now of technical subjects which may well be far beyond the everyday experience of the researcher. In these circumstances the researcher needs detailed background information on the subject, from someone with an expert view, before attempting to design attitudinal (or indeed behavioural) questionnaires.

CLASSIFICATION QUESTIONS

The third group of questions are those used to *classify* the information once it has been collected. Classification questions are required to check that the correct quota of people or companies have been interviewed. They also can be used to validate the sample at the end of the study and make comparisons with the universe as a whole. Not least they are used to compare and contrast the different answers of one group of respondents with those of another. Usually the information that is required for a classification question is behavioural (factual).

Typical classification questions provide a *profile of the respondents* — by finding out their age, their sex, their social class, where they live, their marital status, the type of house they live in, the number of people in their family and so on.

There are a number of standard classification questions which crop up again and again in market research surveys. These are:

■   *Sex.* There can be no other classifications other than male and female.
■   *Household status.* Most researchers classify adults into three groups which are:

    —Head of household   ☐
    —Housewife   ☐
    —Other adult   ☐

■   Marital status. This is usually asked by simply saying 'Are
     you . . . ?'

     —Single   □
     —Married   □
     —Widowed   □
     —Divorced   □
     —Separated   □

■   *Social class.* This is a classification peculiar to UK market
     researchers whereby respondents are pigeonholed according
     to the occupation of the head of the household. Thus, it
     combines the important attributes of income, education
     and work status. Attempts to move market researchers to
     classifications according to income group (as is more com-
     mon in the US) or by lifestyle grouping, have been slow to
     catch on. In summary they are:

     A — Higher managerial, administrative or professional
     B — Intermediate managerial, administrative or profes-
          sional
     C1 — Supervisory, clerical, junior administrative or pro-
          fessional
     C2 — Skilled manual workers
     D — Semi-skilled and unskilled manual workers
     E — State pensioners, widows, casual and lowest grade
          workers.

     For most practical purposes the social classes groupings
     are reduced to just four:

     AB   □
     C1   □
     C2   □
     DE   □

     It is not sufficient to simply have boxes (or numbers) on
     the questionnaire for the interviewer to tick (or circle) to
     indicate the social class of the respondent. There should be
     a line to write in the full occupation since this allows some-
     one at a later stage to see that the response is correct when
     the completed questionnaires are being checked or coded.

■ *Industrial occupation*. Researchers may also want to record the type of firm where the respondent works. In theory it is possible to classify people according to which slot their company falls into within the Standard Industrial Classification (referred to normally as SIC). Researchers often condense the many divisions of the SIC into something which suits their convenience. This could be as simple as:

Primary (farming, forestry, fishing, quarrying etc) ☐
Manufacturing ☐
Retailing and distribution ☐
Service industries ☐
Public service ☐
Armed forces ☐
Education ☐
Professions (doctors, dentists architects etc) ☐

In a consumer survey, it may be relevant to establish the level of employment of the respondent. For example:

Working full-time (over 30 hours a week) ☐
Working part-time (8–30 hours a week) ☐
Housewife (full time at home) ☐
Student (full time) ☐
Retired ☐
Temporarily unemployed (but seeking work) ☐
Permanently unemployed (eg chronically sick, independent means etc) ☐

■ *Number of employees*. The size of the firm in which the respondent works can be important to record — especially in an industrial market research study. Here the conventional classification is:

0–9 ☐
10–24 ☐
25–99 ☐
100–249 ☐
250+ ☐

■ *Location*. The location in which the respondent lives is usually recorded. Depending on the scope of the survey, this can be according to one of the Standard Regions of the UK, ITV reception areas or even a simple split into North, Midlands and South.

■ *Neighbourhood*. Recently there has been a move to group people according to the type of neighbourhood in which they live. These are often referred to as ACORN or PIN-POINT classifications after the market research companies which devised them. They group people into neighbourhood types such as:

Agricultural areas	☐
Modern family houses, higher incomes	☐
Older houses of intermediate status	☐
Poor quality older terraced housing	☐
Better off council estates	☐
Less well off council estates	☐
Poorest council estates	☐
Multi-racial areas	☐
High status, non-family areas	☐
Affluent suburban housing	☐
Better off retirement areas	☐
Unclassified	☐

It should be clear from this consideration of classification questions that the researcher can include many different questions in order to analyse and control the sample. However, a cautionary note is necessary since the purpose of the classification questions may not be fully understood by respondents and there can be many refusals to cooperate in answering them. Rather than build in as many classification questions as possible (just in case they could be useful), the researcher should only include those which are really necessary. Apply the *relevance test* first! Is the information nice to have or necessary to have? What will be done with the information when it has been collected? If the question fails on either of these two counts, it is questionable that it should be asked.

OPEN-ENDED OR CLOSED QUESTIONS AND SCALES

A further variation on behavioural, attitudinal or classification questions is that they can be *open-ended* or *closed*. *Scales* are a special type of closed question.

Open-ended questions, as the name suggests, leave the respondent free to give any answer. Although the question may be asked in open-ended fashion, the researcher may have given thought to the possible answers and have listed a number of alternatives on the questionnaire. These exist for the greater efficiency of completing the questionnaire and the subsequent data processing, and the respondent would be unaware of them. This would be an *open-ended question* but with a *closed answer*.

The second style of question is called a *closed question* and here the replies have been anticipated so that the respondent is asked to choose one or other of the fixed response categories. The pre-defined answers which the researcher has built in to the question will have been worked out by common sense, earlier qualitative research or by a pilot study. The responses would normally be read out (or shown on a card). Thus, closed questions are usually also *prompted questions*.

TABLE 3.2 A CLASSIFICATION OF QUESTION TYPES

	Open ended question	Closed question
Behavioural question	Free response Fixed response	Fixed response
Attitudinal question	Free response Fixed response	Fixed response Scalar response
Classification question	Free response Fixed response	Fixed response

The third style of question is a *scale* — a special type of closed question. Scales could use either words, numbers or even diagrams to find out people's attitudes and behaviour.

Table 3.2 shows the combinations of types of question which could be employed in a questionnaire.

4

FUNDAMENTAL PRINCIPLES OF QUESTIONNAIRE DESIGN

■

Successful questionnaires take the respondent through the interview in such a way that he or she finds it easy to give accurate answers to the questions. Too often questionnaires do not work because the designers *fail to see the questions from the point of view of the respondent.* Bad questionnaires are those where the designer has thought about what is wanted from the survey but where there has been insufficient consideration given to the respondent. This leads to questions which are too long, which are unintelligible (at least to the respondent), and which are too complicated.

Eight rules guide the framing of the questionnaire and these are:

1. think about the objectives of the survey;
2. think about how the interview will be carried out;
3. think about the knowledge and interest of the respondent;
4. think about the introduction;
5. think about the order of the questions;
6. think about the types of questions;
7. think about the possible answers at the same time as thinking about the question;
8. think about how the data will be processed.

THINK ABOUT THE OBJECTIVES OF THE SURVEY

In some surveys, the interview programme is just one part of a multi-faceted study. A variety of research techniques could be involved, each contributing pieces of information to the jigsaw. Desk research, expert interviews, interviews with distributors and interviews with end users, could all play their part. In an eclectic study of this kind, the component parts will have their own separate objectives and the success or otherwise of the whole survey will not depend solely on the interview programme. By limiting the objectives for each part of the survey, and by playing to the strengths of each method which is employed, a questionnaire for an interview programme will not grow too unwieldy since the questions which are within it will only be those relevant to that part of the study.

At the outset, the researcher should sit down with the proposal (the statement of what is to be achieved and the methods which will be involved) and list the objectives appropriate to the interview programme. Firstly, this will ensure that the survey covers all the necessary points and, secondly, it will begin the process of developing a rough topic list which will eventually be converted into more precise questions.

For example, the proposal may state that an objective of the study is to determine what people think of a company and its competitors. The researcher should jot down, in rough, an outline of the questions which will enable the objective to be met, in a simple form such as:

- What is the awareness of the company and its competitors?
- How many people have experience of using the company and its competitors?
- What do they think of the company and its competitors in general terms?
- What do they think of the company and its competitors in specific terms — that is on the quality of its products, the availability of its products, its prices?

Each of these questions opens up more questions and they too should be noted.

■ Which competitors should the company be compared with — all of them or just two or three of the major ones?

■ What does experience of use mean — that a person has bought the product ever? Buys it regularly? Buys it for someone else to use?

■ What do we mean by 'think of the company'? Are we interested in the strengths and weaknesses of firms, or their brands, or both?

■ How do we want people to rate the companies? Should it be in words or on some form of scale?

In this way the researcher brings into focus key words which will help in the framing of the final questions. What is meant by *experience* and *use*? What is meant by *competitors*? What is meant by the word *think*? The thought processes are also turning the researcher's mind towards the possible answers — open-ended comments, fixed responses or scalar ratings.

Frequently, at this stage, the researcher needs to talk again with the person who has commissioned the study to find out exactly what they want.

THINK ABOUT HOW THE INTERVIEW WILL BE CARRIED OUT

At the time of designing the interview programme, the research method will have already been decided. The way the interview will be carried out will have a bearing on the framing of the questions. Face-to-face interviews undertaken by an experienced researcher can cope with more difficult questions than those which would have to be used in a self-completion questionnaire. For example, there is no problem asking open-ended questions in face-to-face interviews while such questions usually generate poor replies in self-completion questionnaires. Questions laid out in a grid (see the examples in the sample questionnaire in Chapter 1) are much more suited to interviews which are administered by a trained researcher but are off-putting in a self-completion questionnaire.

It is worthwhile noting here that the type of researcher or interviewer who will carry out the interviewing will also influence the design of the questionnaire. A skilled and experienced interviewer can make even the worst questionnaire work while a very inexperienced interviewer will need a questionnaire which is buttoned down perfectly with instructions which say clearly what to do now and where to go next.

THINK ABOUT THE KNOWLEDGE AND INTEREST OF THE RESPONDENT

Questions must be within the scope and interest of the respondent. It is not unreasonable for a computer company to want to find out what chief executives think of its (and its competitors') products. However, realistically, how much will the chief executive know and how much time will he be prepared to give to the subject? If it is believed that the chief executive will have only a broad view on computer companies and the performance of their products, then the questions should be framed to capture these general feelings and should not get lost in a tangle of questions which are outside the respondent's experience.

THINK ABOUT THE INTRODUCTION

In street interviews as many as a half of the respondents who are asked to take part in the survey may refuse. In business-to-business surveys over the telephone the refusal rate varies considerably but is frequently around 20 to 30 per cent. The greater the refusal rate, the greater the concern because researchers distrust survey results where the cooperation levels are below 50 per cent. High refusals are costly in terms of time and money but they also can skew a survey if the refusers are in any way different from those who take part. The introduction to a questionnaire can win or lose the respondent and great care should be taken in its construction.

The introduction should make the interview sound interesting and at the same time it should give an explanation as to what it is all about. It may be appropriate in the introduction to provide assurances of confidentiality and to emphasise that there will be no follow-up sales pressure.

Examples of introductions are covered in Chapter 8 which deals with the layout of the questionnaire.

THINK ABOUT THE ORDER OF THE QUESTIONS

An important characteristic of a questionnaire is the sequence of questions. Questions at the beginning of the questionnaire may be designed to check that the right person is being interviewed, perhaps filtering respondents with a peripheral interest in the subject to a special collection of questions. Screening questions may be part of a separate 'recruitment questionnaire' used solely to find suitable respondents before administering the questionnaire proper.

Questions should flow easily from one to another and this is helped if they are grouped into topics which follow a logical sequence, collecting respondents' thoughts in a sensible and orderly way.

In the body of the questionnaire itself, the questions should follow an obvious path and so help the thought processes of respondents. This invariably means moving from the general to the particular; from open-ended questions to closed questions; from unprompted to prompted questions.

Questions should start with those which are relatively easy to answer while the more difficult or threatening ones are left to the end. This enables people to warm to the task of answering, gets them into their stride and prepares them for those questions which are more complex. There is also a build up of confidence during the interview and an associated relaxation on the part of the respondent. This means that there is a greater likelihood that the tricky questions will be answered towards the end of the interview. It would be imprudent to ask the difficult and sensitive questions at the beginning of an interview as there is a strong possibility that they may result in the interview being abandoned.

THINK ABOUT THE TYPES OF QUESTIONS

Long questionnaires which are made up entirely of closed questions and scales can be tedious for respondents who suffer frustration in not being able to express an opinion beyond the fixed choices of responses with which they are presented. Questions which all have the same structure are in danger of placing respondents' minds in a groove. In any case, they can lead to boredom or irritability and neither lead to quality responses. Texture should be given to an interview by building a variety of questions into the questionnaire. The researcher can choose from open-ended questions, closed questions and scales and these are discussed in detail in Chapter 5.

THINK ABOUT THE POSSIBLE ANSWERS AT THE SAME TIME AS THINKING ABOUT THE QUESTION

As the initial questions are roughed out, and with the respondent firmly in mind, the researcher should think about the possible answers which will be received. It may seem presumptuous to attempt to determine answers before the very question itself has been framed, but this process will help tighten up the question. Since the whole purpose of a question is to derive an answer, it is essential that some thought is given to what these answers may be because they may, in turn, influence the shape of the question.

THINK ABOUT HOW THE DATA WILL BE PROCESSED

When the interviewing is complete, the data will require analysing. In a survey involving hundreds of respondents, it is extremely costly to analyse the free-ranging responses to open-ended questions. Where there are hundreds of individual responses, they must be distilled into a much smaller number of groupings in the search for meaningful patterns of response. In order that these replies can be grouped, a coding frame must be developed. This is a short list of cryptic phrases (a dozen at the most) reflecting the essence of the wordy answers. Each open-ended response must then be scrutinised and given a code number which assigns it to one or other of the cryptic phrases so that it can be keyed into the computer for analysis.

Coding is a laborious and expensive process. The answer written on the questionnaire may not make it absolutely clear what the respondent meant — and it is too late to ask for clarification. Making judgements on how to classify the open-ended responses is a potential source of error. All this can be avoided if the answers are pre-empted and listed on the questionnaire ready to be circled during the interview itself. Using forethought or a small number of depth interviews prior to the major study, it should be possible to build a list of most of the alternative answers.

Since data are keyed into a computer as numbers, it makes sense for the response codes also to be numbers which can be circled, as opposed to boxes which are ticked. The example question which follows has not been tested and almost certainly there will be replies beyond those which are listed. These would be recorded on the final line (Others) and can be subsequently coded in the normal way. At least the majority of replies will have been catered for.

Q What are your favourite activities when on holiday? DO NOT PROMPT. CAN MULTI-CODE.

Go on the beach	1 (13)
Swim (not specified where)	2
Sunbathe	3
Play/sit around the pool	4
Sail/windsurf	5
Go for walks/walking	6
Go sightseeing	7
Read books/magazines	8

Have a drink (alcoholic)	9
Go out for meals	10
Play with the children	11
Relax (not specified where)	12
Play sport (any kind)	1 (14)
Meet with friends	2
Do nothing	3
Others (Specify) _____	(15–17)

Most analysis packages emulate one of the first methods of auto-mation used in data processing — the punched card. In the 1950s through to the 1960s a card with 80 columns was punched on a special machine so that when all the cards were stacked together, a needle could be passed through the holes which lined up. The cards with the appropriate answers could then be pulled out and quickly counted. The jargon which originated with the punched card is still used today for describing the method of coding up a questionnaire. The term 'hole count' refers to a straight count of the answers to a question. Data are held in files known as 'cards' and the codes which relate to individual responses are part of a 'column' (the columns are identified by the number in brackets in the above example). Each column has a number and there can be up to 80 columns on a 'card'.

It is necessary that the researcher who designs the question-naire is familiar with the analysis package which will be used. For example, the following information may be required from a respondent:

Q What proportion of the products you buy are sourced from:

	%
Builders merchants	_____
DIY sheds	_____
Other distributors	_____
Direct from manufacturers	_____
TOTAL	**100**

Most computer analysis programmes would cope better with answers to this question if it was laid out thus:

Q What proportion of the products you buy are sourced from:

	Builders merchants (12)	DIY sheds (13)	Other distributors (14)	Direct from manufacturers (15)
0%	1	1	1	1
1–10%	2	2	2	2
11–40%	3	3	3	3
41–65%	4	4	4	4
66–99%	5	5	5	5
100%	6	6	6	6
DK*/Refused	7	7	7	7

*Don't know

Though this layout helps computer analysis, it limits the data since the answers are forced into ranges. In most studies this is acceptable, even desirable, as it removes the necessity for the respondent to be specific. Any calculations can be carried out on the mid-point values of the range.

5

DIFFERENT TYPES OF QUESTIONS

■

In this chapter the focus is on designing questions for *structured* questionnaires. Structured questionnaires are more difficult than semi-structured questionnaires to get right as they must anticipate exactly what people might say and accommodate their answers. Any faults in the wording and design of a question asked of 1000 people will produce results which are unintelligible or misleading and which no amount of statistical processing will be able to rectify. Questionnaires used in large surveys have to be right first time!

GETTING A FEEL FOR THE SUBJECT

It is difficult to design a good questionnaire without becoming steeped in the subject. One of the best ways to do this is to talk about it. If you are to design a questionnaire to find out people's buying habits on hair conditioner, talk about it with your friends. Do they use a conditioner? How often? Who in the family uses the conditioner? Who buys it? Where do they buy it? Do they use a specific brand? What are the benefits of using a conditioner? What are the disadvantages? This type of discussion helps to get into the subject. Points will be raised which may not have been previously considered and which need taking into account in the design of the questionnaire.

If the subject is more esoteric than hair conditioner, it is important to find a knowledgeable person to learn the rudiments. For example, in a survey about batteries for electric fork-lift trucks, it would be helpful in the first instance to speak to a buyer or a maintenance person in a factory where electric fork-lift trucks are used. This pre-questionnaire discussion should not be totally without structure. A short list of the subjects to be covered in the questionnaire should be drawn up to guide this preliminary interview. One of the discussion points with the fork-lift truck respondent, at this early stage, should be about the length of life of the batteries — how variable is it? what affects the length of life? etc. This background enables sensible intervals to be determined for answers to questions.

The researcher must now decide whether to use an open-ended question, one which is closed (ie with a fixed choice) or a scale.

GETTING THE QUESTION STYLE RIGHT — OPEN-ENDED QUESTIONS

An open question is one where the respondent is left free to give any answer and this is either written down verbatim or the interviewer is armed with a list of anticipated pre-defined answers. An example of an open question, closed response would be where the respondent is asked to name brands. This would involve the interviewer in a lot of writing and checking of spelling. If the brands are known, it is far better that they are listed so that the interviewer simply has to circle those mentioned. This speeds up the interview as well as saving time and cost by eliminating the labour of subsequently coding open-ended questions.

In the following example, an open-ended question with a closed response is used as the listing of names is an aid to the interviewer to sort out possible confusion between similar-sounding companies.

Q1   And can I just check whether your company buys any of the following products? READ LIST:

Chain and chain slings	1 →	Q2
Wire rope and wire rope slings	2 →	Q3

| Fibre rope | 3 → Q4 |
| Lifting tackle | 4 → Q5 |

Q2 **FOR THOSE WHO USE CHAIN AND CHAIN SLINGS OF VARIOUS KINDS ASK:** You said that your company buys chain and chain slings. Which companies come to mind as suppliers of chain and chain slings? **DO *NOT* PROMPT. CAN MULTI-CODE.**

Bridon or Bridon Ropes	1
British Ropes	2
Coubro-PCT	3
John Shaw	4
Latch & Batchelor	5
Lifting Gear Hire (LGH)	6
Lifting Gear Products (LGP)	7
Lloyds British	8
Midland Wire Cordage	9
Ropequip	10
Sterling Croft	11
Other **(WRITE IN)** _____	

Two points should be noted about the above question. Firstly, the respondent is likely to know and mention more than one brand (and the question is therefore called multi-response); secondly, a facility is usually provided for additional brands as it is difficult to build a definitive list and someone will always mention a name not listed.

In the previous chapter it has been argued that open-ended questions with open-ended responses should be kept to a minimum in large structured surveys, otherwise they create extra work at the data analysis stage. However, sometimes questions must be asked for which answers cannot be pre-empted or where it is important to capture the exact words which are given in the reply. (Just noting the words that people use in answer to a question can be very revealing).

The example which follows shows an open-ended question which has a lead in from a filter question designed to separate people who have bought a particular product from those who have not. The second part of the question was left open-ended because the range of possible answers was wide and a pre-coded list of responses would have been very lengthy.

Q9A   Did you buy any products as a result of the calls?

Yes	1	**GO TO 9B**
No	2	**SKIP TO 10A**

Q9B   Which products did you buy? PROBE: Any more?

_____

_____

_____

GETTING THE QUESTION STYLE RIGHT —
CLOSED QUESTIONS

Closed questions are so-called because the respondent is asked to choose between a limited number of answers. They are also called *fixed response questions*. The simplest of all closed questions is where there are only two possible answers in which case it known as 'dichotomous'. A typical dichotomous question has the answer 'yes' or 'no'. (In practice there are often cases where 'don't know' is a reasonable alternative).

Closed questions have three main benefits to the researcher:

1.   They save time during the interview because completing the questions simply involves circling numbers.
2.   They assist the respondent because the thinking about the reply options has already been carried out.
3.   Data analysis is made easier as there is no requirement to code up a myriad of open-ended responses.

The following example is a closed question which formed part of a large travel survey involving 500 respondents who were visiting a holiday resort. In a smaller study of 50 to 100 interviews it would have been possible to cope with verbatim responses to an open-ended question but with this larger number it was thought advantageous to close the answers down after a pilot study produced a list of likely responses.

Q   Please look at this card and tell me which statement best describes why you did not use the train for your journey? **SHOW CARD**

Too expensive by train	1
Stations were inconveniently situated	2
Difficult with the luggage	3
Difficult with children	4
Timing not convenient	5
Needed transport to destination	6
Journey takes too long	7
Dislike trains	8
Never thought of going by train	9
Needed a car when I got there	10
Other (specify)	11

Although provision has been left for people to give comments other than those listed on the card, these additional responses will always be under-reported compared with the ones on the list. This is because people's minds are drawn to the easy response, the one which is listed, and only if something is very important to them or startlingly obvious by its omission, will it be mentioned. For this reason it is important to make sure that all the possible responses have been listed.

GETTING THE QUESTION STYLE RIGHT — SCALES

Scales are questions in which the limited choice of response has been chosen to measure an attitude, an intention or some aspect of the respondent's behaviour.

Attitudes or opinions are always important in surveys as they are pointers to people's motivations and, therefore, their likely

buying habits. They can suffer from being over-used and therefore causing frustration to the respondents. It can be soul destroy-
ing, from a respondent's point of view, to answer 20 scalar questions
and not have the opportunity of saying in plain words exactly
how they feel.

My business partner was recently interviewed over the telephone on the subject of computers and was asked dozens of scalar
questions which became boring and seemed irrelevant to his situation. Unfortunately there was no scope to accommodate any
variation from the scales and, following the persistence of the
interviewer, his objective was to bring the unfortunate experience
to a conclusion as quickly as possible. This led him to give any
replies which would satisfy the interviewer since it appeared to
him he could not get out of the interview and there was no
attempt or interest in finding out what he really thought.

The researcher who designed the questionnaire had been
seduced by the attraction of scales. They have the advantage of
pinning a respondent down and forcing a view which, when
pooled with all the other responses, give benchmarks. The analysis
of the results may never expose the fact that many people were
answering in a 'devil may care' fashion as did my partner. Scales
should not be over-used and where they *are* used it should not be
at the expense of restricting people's real views.

The key to designing scalar questions is to decide on what
should be measured and then to determine the appropriate
attributes by which they can be rated. This could involve a small
number of depth interviews before the questionnaire is designed.

There are five different types of rating scales which researchers
commonly use:

1. **Verbal rating scales.** These scales are the simplest of all, in
    which respondents choose a word or phrase on a scale to
    indicate the level of their feeling. The scales usually have
    five choices such as:

    Q   Here is a pack design for a new type of Stilton cheese.
        Please look at it and, using a phrase from this card, tell
        me how appealing you think it is:

Very appealing	1
Quite appealing	2
Neither appealing nor unappealing	3
Quite unappealing	4
Very unappealing	5

A common verbal rating scale asks about people's likelihood of doing something:

Q   And how likely would you be to try this product?

Very likely	1
Quite likely	2
Neither likely nor unlikely	3
Quite unlikely	4
Very unlikely	5

Or the scales may ask the respondent whether or not they agree with a subject or phrase:

Q   I am now going to read out a list of things people have said about these pack designs and I shall ask you which of the phrases on this card best describes how much you agree or disagree with each statement. **READ OUT STATEMENTS. ROTATE ORDER OF START. TICK START.**

	Agree Strongly	Agree Slightly	Neither Nor	Disagree Slightly	Disagree Strongly
This pack looks expensive	1	2	3	4	5
This pack looks modern	1	2	3	4	5
This pack is boring	1	2	3	4	5
This pack is for everyday use	1	2	3	4	5
This pack looks traditional	1	2	3	4	5

2.   **Numerical rating scales.** These have a very similar approach to the verbal rating except that the respondent is asked to give a numerical 'score' rather than a semantic response. The scores are often out of five (where five is best and one

is worst). Ten point scales are sometimes used but they can be more difficult for the respondent as there are more numbers to choose from. A score out of five fits neatly with the five statements on the semantic scale which ranges from very good to very poor and it yields a good distribution of response and enables researchers to easily pick out differences in opinion.

Q   How would you rate the pack on the following?

Very much more convenient   Not at all convenient

5	4	3	2	1

Questions which use numbers for ratings don't have to use scores out of five, nor does the whole scale need to be laid out. The following example is from a self-completion questionnaire and shows how numerical ratings can be an economical means of laying out rating questions. The numbers in brackets at the end of each line are column numbers for use in the data analysis.

Q   Below are two columns of descriptions which some people have used to describe what influences their choice of cars. The first column contains general descriptions of cars. The second column contains descriptions which could be applied to the inside of a car. Look through each of the columns of descriptions and tell us how important you think each factor is to you, when making your choice. Give each description a score out of ten — where ten is *very important* and one is *not important at all.*

GENERAL DESCRIPTIONS

Roomy	____ (7)	Sporty appearance	____ (15)
Large	____ (8)	Stylish	____ (16)
Functional	____ (9)	Distinctive	____ (17)
Safe	____ (10)	Classy looking	____ (18)
Suitable for families	____ (11)	Contemporary looking	____ (19)
Versatile	____ (12)	Well specified	____ (20)
Well built	____ (13)		
Small	____ (14)		

DESCRIPTIONS OF THE INTERIOR

A modern interior ...... ____ (21)   Light & airy.................. ____ (26)
Hard wearing   Practical......................... ____ (27)
  materials .... ____ (22)   Comfortable................. ____ (28)
Attractive colours .... ____ (23)   Good boot capacity ... ____ (29)
Roomy........................... ____ (24)   Easy to load.................. ____ (30)
Good ergonomics....... ____ (25)

3. **The use of adjectives.** A variation on the verbal/semantic scale is to ask respondents which words best describe a company, a product or, as in the next example, a person. The adjectives could be a mixture of both positive and negative and they need not be opposites.

Q I would like to read out some words which describe people. You have to choose one word from each pair to describe yourself. If you think neither fits, you must choose the one which is closest. Would you say that you are ....

Introvert	1	or extrovert	2
Traditionalist	1	or an experimenter	2
Stylish	1	or fashionable	2
Ambitious	1	or content	2
Independent	1	or gregarious	2
Intellectual	1	or practical	2

4. **The use of positioning statements.** The respondent is asked to agree or disagree with a number of statements. It is important that the respondent is readily able to identify with one of the statements and is not left feeling that in certain circumstances one would apply and in other circumstances the other would be more appropriate.

Q This next question is simply to help us group your reply along with others of a similar type. I will read out some statements which people have said about the xxx car. Would you give me a score out of five to say whether you agree or disagree with the statement? A score of one means you disagree strongly. **SCORE 6 FOR DON'T KNOW.**

	Agree strongly			Disagree strongly		Don't know
A car that is a pleasure to look at	5	4	3	2	1	6
A car I hope says something to others about me	5	4	3	2	1	6
A car that is distinctive but not flashy	5	4	3	2	1	6
A rational choice of car	5	4	3	2	1	6
An emotional choice of car	5	4	3	2	1	6
The cheapest suitable car I could find	5	4	3	2	1	6
A car I enjoy driving fast	5	4	3	2	1	6
A car that doesn't attract too much attention	5	4	3	2	1	6
A car with a happy personality of its own	5	4	3	2	1	6
A car that tells people I'm different	5	4	3	2	1	6

5. **Ranking questions.** A way to find out what is most important to a respondent is to present a number of factors and ask which is most important, which is second most important and so on. Show cards should be used where possible to present the factors. However, to remove any bias in the order in which they are presented, the factors could each be printed on a different card so that they can be shuffled. If this is likely to prove difficult (for example in street interviews) the interviewers could have a number of cards on which the factors are presented in a varying order. In ranking questions it is usually not valid to ask respondents to rank beyond the top three factors. This is because the less important factors become, the more they tend to merge in the minds of the respondents and the harder it is to assign a level of rank.

    Q   I will now show you a card on which is listed a number of factors which could be important to you when choosing a combined weedkiller and fertiliser. Would you look at the list and tell me which is the most important factor in influencing your choice? **READ LIST. ROTATE START. TICK START. RANK JUST THREE FACTORS.**

And what would be the second most important factor?

And what would be the third most important factor?

FACTOR	RANK
Available in the garden centre	_____
A competitive price	_____
Works at any time of year	_____
Kills weeds *and* moss	_____
Not poisonous to children or pets	_____
Made by a well known company	_____

Ranking questions that are read out must not be too long otherwise the respondents will forget what has been said.

Sometimes respondents are asked to rank the first two most important factors and the least important. However, this is not really necessary as the least important factor can always be determined at the analysis stage, being the one which receives the fewest number of first, second or third rankings.

6

FRAMING THE QUESTIONS

■

GETTING THE WORDS RIGHT

Choosing one or other of the three styles of questions (open, closed or scales), the researcher can now frame the words that will be asked. It will be assumed that the key areas of information required from the study have been listed and that some feel for the subject has been obtained from discussions with people who buy or use the product.

Here are four important questions the researcher should ask when drafting a question:

1. Will this question be understood in the way that I intend?
2. How many different ways could this question be interpreted?
3. Is this question likely to annoy or offend?
4. Is there a better way of asking the question?

Don't expect the draft of a question to be right first time. Think about the way questions are posed in ordinary conversation. Frequently in conversation you need to obtain further clarification as to what was intended by the question. Was the question clear? Was it necessary to add a rider to the first question, having listened to the answer? Is there still a possibility that the question has not been fully understood?

In a market research study involving many interviews, there is no scope for debate about what was really meant by the question. Its meaning needs to be clear straight away.

DO'S AND DON'TS IN THE WORDING OF QUESTIONS

During the drafting of the words of the questions the researcher is looking for clarity and this is achieved by following a number of simple rules:

■ *Ensure that the question is without bias.* One of the most frequent and serious errors in the wording of questions is the introduction of bias. Very often the bias is unintentional but it creeps in nevertheless. An obvious use of bias is the presentation of a question in such a way as to lead the respondent into the answer. For example, 'Would you agree that the company has an excellent product range?' The question becomes more impartial if some counter weight is introduced. 'Would you agree or disagree that the company has an excellent product range?' However, there is still bias within the question because the idea has been implanted in the respondent's mind that the product range is excellent by the very use of that word. Reducing the bias still further the question could be asked:

Q   Would you say the Company's product range is:

Very good	1
Quite good	2
Neither good nor bad	3
Quite poor	4
Very poor	5

Researchers may still argue that the very act of presenting the scale from positive to negative has some bias and that the order of the scale should be rotated. They may even say that it is better to use the word 'good' throughout so that in the negative part of the scale the terms 'Not very good' and 'Not at all good' are used instead of 'Quite poor' and 'Very poor'.

Erudite papers are written by researchers on the bias which can be introduced by these issues. Is there a bias in a blind taste test in favour of product labelled X or one labelled Y? Is there a bias in favour of scales which have the positive attributes at the top or the bottom? Is there a bias in favour of scales in which people have to choose one of two attributes where the positive attributes are to the left and the negative ones to the right?

All these factors have been shown to cause bias to varying degrees, but it is usually quite small and has much less effect than does poor sampling or bad interviewing. The researcher is encouraged to think carefully about the wording of all questions to eliminate as much bias as possible, but not to develop a neurosis which makes them too nervous to put pen to paper.

■ *Jargon or shorthand may not be understood by the respondent.* It cannot be assumed that respondents will understand words which are in common usage to the researcher. Marketing and trade jargon, acronyms and initials which shorten everyday conversations may not be universally familiar. Even some words or phrases in everyday use can give rise to confusion. For example, when speaking to buyers one has to be very clear as to what precisely is meant by the terms 'margin' and 'mark-up'. In the same way, terms such as 'Gross Domestic Product', 'purchasing criteria', and 'marque' can create problems for respondents.

■ *Steer clear of sophisticated or uncommon words* (eg 'salient', 'rancour', 'synergy'). A questionnaire is not a place to score literary points so, if in doubt, keep it simple. Be prepared to use colloquialisms if they are more meaningful, for example, in some areas in the North of England it may be necessary to refer to bread rolls as 'baps', this being the familiar terminology. However it is important to use words which all respondents can understand and so if the bread survey was carried out nationally, there would have to be alternative definitions for other regions.

■ *Avoid ambiguous words.* You may know what you mean by 'usually' but will the respondent? The word 'frequently' would be acceptable in a question which asked: 'How frequently do you buy instant coffee?' but it would lack precision if it was rephrased: 'Do you frequently buy instant coffee?'

■ *Make the question as short as possible.* A very long question can lose the respondent partway through. Sometimes the researcher has a burning need to put a question into a context to give it meaning. This can be necessary in certain circumstances. Respondents may need reminding of an event or require some explanation before an answer can be given. The following example reminds or informs people about something which is critical to answering the question:

> 'The Chancellor in his autumn statement said that the economy was showing signs of improvement and could be expected to grow at three per cent over the next year. Would you agree or disagree with this view?'

However, sometimes questions get out of hand:

> 'In the light of the most recent inflation figures and bearing in mind the Chancellor's autumn statement, what do you think are the prospects for your business over the next year?'

This may be better asked as 'How is business right now?'

■ *Make the question as simple as possible.* Following on from the above point, questions should not only be short, they should also be simple. Questions which include multiple ideas will be confusing to the respondent and the answer could be unintelligible. For example, the question 'When you buy both aluminium *and* steel strip, do you use a different supplier?' was found in a questionnaire and is bogged down with multiple ideas.

Similarly, it is easy to fall into the trap of building two questions into one, for example 'Did you drive or did your partner?' If a question looks as if it is becoming too complicated, it may be because it justifies being split into two separate questions.

■ *Make the questions very specific.* Again the rule is for brevity and simplicity. However, there are occasions when it is advisable to lengthen the question by adding memory cues — such as 'Have you, yourself, bought any xxx in the last three months; I mean in September, October or November?' There are two memory cues in this question. Firstly a reminder that the question relates to the respondent personally and, secondly, that the last three months comprised September, October and November.

It is always good practice to be specific with time periods. For example don't be vague about 'last year' — spell out whether this means the last twelve months or the last full year from January to December. Remember that there is a temptation for people to extend periods rather than contract them. Pinning down the dates reduces the chances of 'over-claiming' in the responses.

■ *Make sure that the question and answer do not conflict.* There is a danger that in trying to make a question clearer the result could become confusing, for example 'Do you care what brand you buy or would you buy any brand?'

■ *Keep the number of meaningful words to a minimum.* Questions which include a number of profound words could bamboozle and the researcher would be unsure which word swayed the response. The following question is rather heavy in its use of meaningful words: 'What motivates and inspires you in the selection or specification of a new supplier?' Once more, simplicity rules and a better question may be, 'What, above all else, influences your choice of a new supplier?'

■ *Avoid questions with a negative in them.* Questions are more difficult to understand if they are asked in a negative sense. It is better to say 'Are you likely to buy XXX in the next three months?' than to say 'Are you not likely to buy . . . ?'; 'Do you ever . . . ?' as opposed to 'Do you never . . . ?'

■ *Avoid hypothetical questions.* It has been reported that when Xerox commissioned research on the potential for its new copying process, the consultants forecast demand for 8000 units over six years while, in the event, Xerox installed

80,000 units in three years. The consultants were seeking answers to questions people could not really give as there is a conditioning process which affects people's actions in the longer run. Nevertheless, researchers frequently are under pressure to ask hypothetical questions knowing that the results cannot be trusted.

■ *Do not use words which could be misheard.* This is especially important over the telephone. For example the numbers 15 and 50 can be misheard, so if these *must* be used it would be wise to also spell them out — ie '15, I mean one five; 50 I mean five oh'.

■ *Do not offer fixed alternatives which could both be valid.* Attitudinal questions can sometimes be irritating to respondents if they feel that their answer is being forced into a box which does not reflect reality. In the following example there is no provision for the fact that the drink could taste both sour and bitter:

Q   Would you say that the drink tasted: sour . . . bitter?
                                              1   2

■ *Keep questions within the respondents' capabilities.* A question which asked distributors of clutches how many they sold per year obtained a poor response because the distributors held figures in their heads on monthly, not annual, sales. When the question was changed the question was answered with very little trouble.

■ *Desensitise questions by using response bands.* Questions which ask ladies about their age or companies about their turnover are best asked in bands. The respondent is less inclined to think that confidences are being divulged if the response categories are fairly broad. Since the data will almost certainly be grouped into bands at the analysis stage, it may as well be collected as such. Thus:

I will read out a number of turnover bands and would you tell me which your company fits into:

Less than £1 million	1
£1 million to £10 million	2

Over £10 million to £50 million   3
Over £50 million   4 Please specify _____

In a situation such as that above the respondent may well
be asked to be more specific if his turnover is more than
£50 million as the data may be required to work out aver-
ages and gross up. Without some specific figures on the
'over £50 million' respondents, the average of this band
would be impossible to calculate.

■ *Make it easy for respondents to answer questions.* Developing
   the above point further, it is easier for a respondent to
   answer a numeric question within bands than to answer
   specifically. If you do not need the answer to be specific,
   make the respondent's task easier by banding the responses.
   For example, the question 'How much did you spend in
   XXX's supermarket last week?' would have people racking
   their memories for the exact figure when you may be quite
   satisfied to know the figure within £10 bands. If this is the
   case the respondent should be prompted with those bands.
   That is:

Was it . . .   Nothing   1
               Less than £10   2
               £10 to £20   3
               £21 to £30   4
               Etc

It should be noted that in a question such as this, the people
who do not shop in XXX's supermarket would normally be
rerouted so that they are not asked how much they spent. It
is still prudent, however, to make provision for someone
who passed the routing, perhaps because they normally
shop at XXX, but for one reason or another they did not
spend anything there in the relevant week. This requires
the response category 'nothing' which is a very different
answer to 'less than £10'.

Some work may have to be done prior to designing the
questionnaire to find suitable intervals for the bands. For
example, if a researcher had to design a questionnaire
aimed at collecting data on distributors' sales of commer-

cial brake linings, it would be necessary first to speak to a few distributors to find out sensible turnover bands.

■ *Allow for 'others' in fixed response questions.* Pre-coded lists, which are not read out and which are for the convenience of the interviewers and the coders, should always have provision for responses other than those which are listed. If the list of responses is read out, once again there should be provision for answers which have not been included but it should be realised that these 'other' responses will always be under-recorded.

■ *Ensure that fixed responses do not overlap.* The categories which are used in a fixed-response question should be sequential but not overlap otherwise there will always be someone who is caught on the cusp.

■ *Consider 'softening' knowledge-based questions.* If it is necessary to ask a respondent whether they know the date a magazine was launched, or the name of products they last bought, or the price they paid, it may soften the question to insert a phrase such as 'Can you recall offhand . . . ?' or 'Do you happen to know . . . ?'

■ *Consider using projective questions where the subject is sensitive or difficult.* There are circumstances when people may not like to admit that they act in a certain way. Sometimes they may not even recognise why they act or think as they do. These may be occasions for moving the question beyond the respondent and into a wider frame. For example, prior to asking a company about the prices it is paying for a product, it could be better to lead with a question about the market as a whole. It will help make way for the more sensitive questions.

QXa Thinking about companies like yours, what would you say are typical of the prices they pay for ground bar?

£_____/tonne

QXb And would you say that the price your company pays is higher or lower than this?

Higher   1 → How much higher?   _____ %
The same   2
Lower   3 → How much lower?   _____ %

7

INTERVIEWER INSTRUCTIONS

■

KEEPING A RECORD OF CONTACTS

In most surveys it is important to keep a tally of who has been contacted when attempting to achieve the interviews. Street interviews are an exception as usually the interviewer keeps a count of the people interviewed only as a match against the quota which is being sought. In most other circumstances, interviewers either have to find an appropriate respondent or are given a list of people to interview and the *contact sheet* provides a useful mechanism for keeping orderly records on the resulting success or otherwise.

The contact sheet (see following example) does a number of things:

■ It is a means of distributing work to a number of interviewers as the names of companies or people to interview can be written on each sheet.

■ It is somewhere to write down details on respondents who are being tracked down but where the details of the interview have yet to be confirmed. In most studies it is reasonable to try up to three times to get hold of a respondent and each occasion should be at a different time and date (unless, of course, a special arrangement has been made). These details could be written onto the questionnaire itself or on separate pieces of paper but it is usually better to keep all the interview planning information together so

Job Number:					Project Name:	
Respondent's name	Address	Date/time of calling			Result	
		1st call	2nd call	3rd call	Interview (tick)	Reason for non-interview

that it can be easily referred to and subsequently analysed (see the next point).

■ At the end of a study the researcher may want to see what proportion of the contacts resulted in an interview and how many failed because of refusal to participate, inappropriateness, non-contactibility etc. This information on 'strike rates' may have a direct input in the survey. For example, from contact sheets it would be possible to calculate how many people or companies use a product and how many do not (the latter being inappropriate for interview) and this proportion may have considerable value in the study.

Calculating the response rates on studies is also of importance in gauging the robustness of the sample. Where the strike rate of interviews is around the 50 per cent mark or lower (after stripping out the non-eligible respondents) the researcher should become concerned about the representativeness of the sample. In most studies a strike rate of around 60 to 80 per cent would be considered reasonable and this can be determined from the contact sheets.

LAYING OUT THE INSTRUCTIONS

Questionnaires are usually administered by someone other than their designer. The interviewer (or in the case of self-completion questionnaires, the respondent him- or herself), needs clear guidance what to do at every stage. These instructions need to be differentiated from the text either by capital letters, emboldened or underlined type. There are no rigid conventions in the industry and researchers can choose any style of differentiating instructions they like. However, it is helpful if the instructions are in a consistent format within the same questionnaire so that the interviewer becomes familiar with them.

We have already seen a number of examples of instructions in questions. The following example is typical:

Q10A   I will now read out some factors which may have influenced your choice of the Prelude. After I have read them out would you tell me which was most important in causing you to put the Prelude on your shopping list.
ROTATE LIST, FACTORS 1–6. TICK START

Q10B   And what was second in importance?

	10A First Mention	10B Second Mention
An advert	1	1
Recommendation	2	2
A road test report	3	3
Previous ownership of a Prelude	4	4
Previously driven or been a passenger in a Prelude	5	5
Seen the Prelude when driving about	6	6
Other _____		

In the above example there are two important instructions. The first is that the interviewer is told to rotate the order of the list of factors, otherwise there would be a danger that the first factor will turn out to be mentioned most frequently in view of its privileged position in the listing. The second instruction tells the interviewer to tick the place at which the rotation started. This is as a reminder to the interviewer to rotate and it acts as a check for the researcher who is controlling the study.

THE INTRODUCTION

The introduction to the interview is critical in winning the interest and cooperation of the respondent and to ensure that the right person has been obtained for questioning. It is not good enough to leave this to the interviewers, no matter how well briefed. The researcher needs to think through the precise way the interview should be introduced and produce a script which is part of the questionnaire.

The introduction aims to do three things:

1. Set the scene so that the respondent knows what is happening. It would be stated that the interview is for market research purposes only and frequently it is appropriate to give assurances of confidentiality.
2. Engage the interest of the respondent. The study will be all the more accurate if it has a high response rate and the introduction is the opportunity to 'sell it in'.
3. Ensure that the right person has been chosen for interview. Since good research is about asking the right question of the right person, this is the point at which to check that the right person has been selected.

In theory the introduction should be administered as quickly as possible as it is advantageous to move the respondent straight into interviewing mode. Once the questions have started, people rarely give up. Introductions have to be made over the telephone, in the street or on a doorstep and in these conditions it can stretch the respondent's patience to spend too much time explaining the whys and wherefores. A balance needs to be struck between covering all the issues and getting down to questioning in the shortest possible time.

Below is an example of an introduction which was used in a survey carried out amongst buyers of Honda Prelude cars. The interview was administered by telephone and was part of a study covering ten countries.

HONDA PRELUDE STUDY

ASK TO SPEAK TO THE PRINCIPAL DRIVER OF THE PRELUDE. THE INTERVIEW MUST BE WITH THE PRINCIPAL DRIVER. Hello. My name is .... and I am from Business & Market Research, an international market research company working for Honda. It is part of Honda's policy to speak to a sample of car owners to find out what they think about Honda cars. I understand that you have recently bought a Prelude. Can I check that you are the principal driver? I would appreciate it if you could help me with a few simple questions. It will take around 15 minutes and any replies you give will be totally confidential. Only the pooled analysis will be passed to Honda. Thank you. First of all can I confirm that you had a major influence on the choice of the Prelude? **IF NOT, THANK AND CLOSE.**

Q1 Which model of Prelude did you eventually buy? **CLARIFY MODEL TO PRINCIPAL DRIVER, CONFIRM STATUS, RE-ROUTE OR CLOSE.**

2.0 EX	1
2.0 EX Classic	2
2.0 EX 4 Wheel Steer (4WS)	3
2.0i 16	4
2.0i 16 4WS	5
2.0i 16 4WS SE	6
2.0i 16 Classic	7
Other _____	

Following the introduction, the first question in a survey should be simple and straightforward for the respondent. In the above case, everyone was able to state the model of car they had bought and the question clicked people's minds into thinking about the subject of the investigation.

ROUTING

Unless stated otherwise, the interviewer will proceed from question to question. However, there will be frequent occasions when an answer to a certain question requires a special line of further questioning which is not appropriate for everyone. The interviewer is directed to the next question by an instruction which is known as a *routing*, a *filter* or a *skip*. The key to successful routing is to take the respondent swiftly and smoothly to the next question without a break or hesitation.

As with all the instructions in the questionnaire, there should be some common convention in type style and it is usual to use capitals.

Q47   Thank you very much, that has been very helpful. Let me tell you that this survey is being sponsored by Johnson Matthey. Have you ever dealt with the company?

Yes   1   ASK Q48
No   2   SKIP TO Q50

Questions 48 and 49 in the survey addressed respondents who had used Johnson Matthey and asked how long it was since they had dealt with the company and who they had dealt with. In question 50 everyone came back together, irrespective of whether they had dealt with Johnson Matthey, and were asked what they thought of the company.

PROBING

Free-ranging responses to open-ended questions are sometimes lacking in depth or require further explanation to be meaningful. For example, the question 'What do you think of Johnson

Matthey as a company?' may solicit the answer 'Very good, I like them.' This may tell us that Johnson Matthey is considered in a good light but that is about all we have learned. An explanation is needed as to *why*. Interviewers are taught to probe deeper following all open-ended responses using further questions such as:

- Why did you say that?
- Is there anything else?
- What made you say that?
- Tell me more about that?
- That is interesting, what lies behind your answer?

And in response to a question which asked for the recall of something — such as names of companies, brands, or points which were remembered in an advert:

- Any others?

The interviewer instruction would be in capitals and may simply say PROBE.

> Q55 What, above all else, comes to mind when you think of Johnson Matthey? **PROBE**.

Sometimes there are issues which it is hoped will come out in open-ended questioning but, should this not be the case, they can be teased out with specific probes. For example:

> Q42 What do you think of the company for its deliveries? **PROBE** reliability of deliveries, speed of deliveries.

PROMPTS

Prompting is not the same as probing. A prompt suggests a possible answer to the respondent whereas a probe remains open-ended. Prompts are used in pre-coded questions where the response categories are fixed. They would normally be read out or shown on a card. It is important that the interviewer is clear whether the pre-coded answers are there to be used as prompts or if they are simply there for interviewing and data processing convenience. In the two questions which follow, the first is not prompted and the second one is:

Q   What is the reason for your visit to Marple today? DO NOT PROMPT.

Work	1
Shopping	2
Visiting friends/relations etc	3
Looking around/passing through	4
To eat/drink	5
Car service	6
Medical/dentist	7
Sport/recreational	8
Other _____	

Q And how do you like the town? READ SCALE.

Like it a lot	1
Quite like it	2
Not very keen on it	3
Don't like it at all	4

By way of illustration, the above scale shows that there is no formality to their wording and any phrases can be used which the researcher thinks is appropriate for capturing the mood of the answer. Nor is it necessary for all scales to have a mid and neutral point (although they usually do). Sometimes researchers deliberately miss these out so that it forces an opinion towards one or other of the poles.

When questioning the recall of brands or names of companies it is normal to ask the question in open-ended fashion first and then to prompt as illustrated in the following example:

Q2a   I would like you to think about pharmaceutical wholesalers. Which names come to mind? DO NOT PROMPT. PROBE: Any others?

Q2b   And now I would like to read out a list of names of

pharmaceutical wholesalers. As I read out each name would you tell me if you have heard of the company? **READ LIST. ROTATE START. TICK START.**

	Q2a	Q2b
Ayrton Saunders	1 (8)	1 (10)
Butlers	2	2
Daniels (Richard)	3	3
Foster (George)	4	4
Harris (Philip)	5	5
Hills	6	6
Macarthy	7	7
Mawdsleys	8	8
Rowlands	9	9
Sants Pharmac.	10	10
SOT/Barclay	11	11
UniChem	12	12
Vestric	1 (9)	1 (11)
None	2	N/A
Others (specify) _____		

MULTI-CODING

In the previous example a respondent would almost certainly have been aware of a number of pharmaceutical companies. The question made it clear that as many names as possible were being sought. This is a multi-response question in which the interviewer would circle as many names as are recalled. Sometimes it may not be clear as to whether multi- or single responses are acceptable and an instruction should be provided.

Q In order that we can classify the answers you have just given me, would you tell me the principal nature of your company's business? **DO NOT PROMPT. CIRCLE ONLY ONE ANSWER.**

Civil engineers	1
Building contractors	2
Process engineers	3

Process plant suppliers   4
Consulting engineers   5
Quantity surveyors   6
Architects   7
Others _____

Q And which of the following territories accounts for most of your overseas work? **PROMPT WITH LIST. ROTATE LIST. TICK START. CAN ACCEPT MORE THAN ONE RESPONSE.**

Europe other than the UK   1
North America   2
South America   3
Middle East   4
Far East   5
Africa   6
Australasia   7
Soviet/CIS bloc   8
Others _____

In examples such as these it will be clear that some clarification or qualification to an answer may be needed. The interviewer needs to know what to do if the respondent says they design process plant. Is the company to be slotted in with 'Consulting engineers', 'Process engineers' or 'Process plant suppliers'? And what should they do if a respondent says they are involved in a major project in Turkey — is this to be classified within Europe or the Middle East? These types of problems arise in interviews and they can be catered for by a thorough briefing of the interviewing team.

8

THE LAYOUT OF THE QUESTIONNAIRE

■

A questionnaire is a *working* document. It presents the questions as well as the place and space to record the answers. Thought needs to be given to ensure that the layout of the questions and the questionnaire as a whole enable it to work.

FORMALITIES ON EVERY QUESTIONNAIRE

Every questionnaire should have a title which enables it to be readily identified. Some market research companies give each job a number or code and this too may be recorded on the questionnaire. And, to state the obvious, the place for the title is at the top of the page. Within my own company the top of each questionnaire has a number of boxes for department heads to say that they have seen and approved the questionnaire. In the header, PM stands for Project Manager, DP for data processing, and SM for show material.

At the foot of the page is a declaration for the interviewer to sign and confirm that the interview has been carried out within the Market Research Society's Code of Practice. The following template is only shown by way of example and every researcher should decide what is necessary and relevant for their company.

Questionnaires should also have provision to record the name and address of the respondent, the date of the interview and the name of the interviewer. This data can be recorded at the beginning

| Columns 1-4 | | Column 5 | 1 | Job No [1992] (Columns 6 -8) | 4 | 1 | 5 |

| Module | I | Designer JC | PM Check JC | Client Approved ✓ | Phone Check N/A |
| Field Check SL | DP Check DE | SM Check ✓ | Anticipated Interview Duration: 25 .. minutes |

Business & Market Research Plc, Buxton Road, High Lane, Stockport, SK6 8DX. Telephone: (0663) 765115

Project Louis

Respondent Details

Name: ....

Address: ....

....

....

Occupation of Head of Household: ....

Qualifications: ....

No. of Persons Resp. for: ....

Classification

SEG	(9)	Age	(11)	Presence of Children	(13)
AB	1	25-34	1	With children under 16	1
C1	2	35-45	2	No children under 16	2
C2DE	CLOSE				

Sex	(10)	Location	(12)
Male	1	Bracknell	1
Female	2	Uxbridge	2
		Altrincham	3

I declare that this interview was carried out according to instructions, within the MRS Code of Practice and that the respondent was not previously known to me.

Name: .... Signature: ....

Date: .... Actual Interview Duration: .... minutes or at the end of the questionnaire depending on preference and circumstances. In the case of business-to-business interviews it is normal to have the name and address at the front of the questionnaire so that when all the interviews are completed, a company can easily be located by looking through the top sheets. In street interviews the respondent's name and address is usually the last thing to be asked and so this is positioned at the end of the questionnaire.

The following is typical of a 'boilerplate' for an industrial questionnaire:

STRUCTURAL STEELWORK STUDY
Project Number: 087 92/I

Name of company: _____

Address: _____

_____

_____

Telephone Number: _____

Contact — Name: _____

Contact — Position: _____

Interviewer: _____

Date: _____

MAKING THE LAYOUT SUITABLE FOR THE FIELD

If ever there is a conflict between laying out a questionnaire for the convenience of data processing, the finance department or the field interviewers, it is the latter who should win every time. They have to make the questionnaire work.

Space is at a premium in a questionnaire and should be used wisely. If the questionnaire is too cramped it will be hard to read and difficult to write down the answers. If space is used too freely the questionnaire will grow and become book-like, unwieldy and expensive to print.

Make sure that the size of the type is large enough to be read in the conditions where the interview may have to be administered — at worst, a murky street in winter, or a doorstep with poor lighting; at best an office floodlit with fluorescent lights.

There should be sufficient space for the interviewer to record the answers and this is especially important for open-ended questions. It should also be borne in mind that the number of lines for the answer is some indication to the interviewer of the length of response which is expected. The next example has been taken from a self-completion questionnaire completed by fleet buyers who took part in a 'clinic'. The fact that only one line is allowed for each factor indicates that a word or two is all that is called for.

Q   Now, taking into consideration those factors you have just rated, but also pulling in any others you feel may be relevant, what are the three most important things you look for in a fleet car?

Number 1 in importance: _____

Number 2 in importance: _____

Number 3 in importance: _____

And in an administered questionnaire on the subject of banking, the interviewer was able to gauge the depth of response from the space allowed for the answer:

Q   Just so that I am clear, what was the single most important factor which resulted in you choosing your principal bank? **PROBE**.

_____

_____

USING GRIDS

The researcher should become accustomed to thinking about efficient ways of recording the answers. Sometimes grids can be helpful. A grid lays out the responses across and down as is shown in the sample questionnaire in Chapter 1.

LAYOUT FOR DATA PROCESSING

A questionnaire which is part of a large sample will require data processing and it will be necessary to think of how to record the answers to save time and costs at the analysis stage. The researcher should discuss the layout of the questionnaire with data processing staff at the outset. Most data processing packages use column numbers for recording the individual responses and typically these would be laid out in a manner similar to the many examples which have been used so far. The column numbers in the following self-completion example have been placed at the head of the column.

This section asks for some details on yourself which will help us classify your answers.

1 Your age:	(7)	2 Your sex:	(8)
20 or under	1	Male	1
21–24	2	Female	2
Over 25	3		

3 Your faculty:

(9)

Art & Design   1
Comm studies & Ed   2
Hollings   3
Human, Law & Soc Sci   4
Mangmt & Business   5
Science & Engineering   6
Other   7

4 Your home before com-
   ing to the college:

(10)

North West   1
South West   2
Yorkshire & Humberside   3
London & South East   4
West Midlands   5

East Midlands   6
Elsewhere in UK   7
Europe (not UK)   8
Africa   9
Far East   10
Elsewhere in the world   11

5 The qualification for which
   you are studying:

(11)

Degree   1
Post Graduate   2
Diploma in Higher
   Education   3
HND   4
Higher & Research   5
Professional/other   6

Sometimes data processing departments appreciate a column set aside for writing numbers and codes at the time the questionnaires are processed. This may look as follows:

SUBJECT FLOW

The importance of 'flow' in the questionnaire has already been stressed a number of times. Achieving good flow means grouping questions into blocks which relate to a subject before moving on to another, closely connected, subject. It means moving in a logical sequence from one subject to another, from broad issues to narrower ones and from open-ended questioning to prompted questioning. In broad terms the following sequence would be sensible for a study testing the use of and attitudes to a product.

16 July 1992 : Boo 9099

26b	**ASK IF YES AT Q26a** What proportion of these patients are given an ACE inhibitor?

_____ %   (44–46)

(write in %)

26c What are your feelings about prescribing ACE inhibitors in
this situation?

_____

_____

_____   (47–49)

26d If there were a viable therapeutic alternative to an ACE
inhibitor in this situation, would you consider prescribing it?   (50–52)

_____

26e What would be the desirable characteristics of such an
alternative drug?   (53–55)

_____

27a What is your usual next step for patients who are symptomatic
on their current therapy and for whom ACE inhibitors are
inappropriate therapy? Do you (**READ OUT**)   (56)

         refer patient to another doctor   1 → Q.28
         prescribe an ACE inhibitor   2 → Q.28
         prescribe another drug   3 → Q.27b
         take other action   4 → Q28
         – Specify

ASK IF ANOTHER DRUG IS PRESCRIBED
27b Which alternative drug do you prescribe most often in this
situation?

_____

    (57–59)

Grouping Questions Into Blocks Which Flow

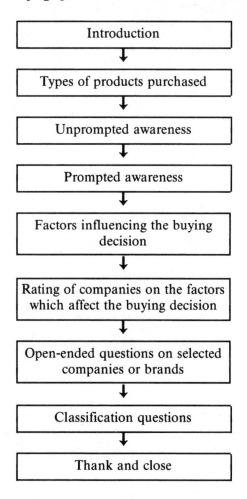

THE USE OF BRIDGING STATEMENTS

It can sometimes help the continuity of a questionnaire if there are links between the groups of questions. Examples of bridging statements are:

Thank you, I would now like to move on to the subject of . . .
That was helpful. We now turn to . . .
I have a complete change of subject for you now . . .

It can assist the flow to include encouraging statements in the questions themselves with the caveat that they should not be overused, abused or made to sound patronising. They are simple courtesies which make the interview a little more 'user friendly':

You are doing fine.
Thank you for your patience.
Just a few more questions now.
We'll soon be finished.

Towards the end of the interview there will be the need to ask classification questions. The relevance of these may not be apparent to the respondent and yet there is no time for a full explanation as to why they are needed. It can ease the way in by saying:

We are nearly at the end now. In order that we can classify the answers you have given us I wonder if you tell me some details about you and your family. Can I start with . . . ?

SHOW CARDS

A show card (sometimes called a prompt card) is used to present a list of words, statements, names or concepts to a respondent as an aid to the questioning. The show card is so called because of the instruction which is placed on the questionnaire ('SHOW CARD') and tells the interviewer when to use it. They are frequently used in face-to-face consumer interviews in the street and home. They can also be used in business-to-business telephone interviews if an initial call confirms cooperation, after which the show cards are posted or faxed to the respondent, ready for the follow up call.

The information on the card acts as a reminder so that scales, long phrases or lists of names do not need reading out or repeating. Cards are useful for communicating pictures of products, banner headings of newspapers, logos of companies — images which would be difficult to describe verbally or which would somehow be lacking if they were not shown in total.

Show cards can be useful for controlling the interview. The words on the cards can be rotated with each interviewer having a different version and so removing this task from their responsibility. If a number of cards are to be used, they can be kept in order by being tied in the corner by string or comb bound into a small book.

COMPLETING THE INTERVIEW

When the interview is finished it must be closed down in a courteous and professional manner. It may be appropriate to restate the promise of confidentiality which was made at the beginning or to give an assurance of the fact that the interview was for market research purposes only.

An example of a conclusion to a telephone interview is:

'Thank you for your help. It is much appreciated. Can I remind you that this was a bona fide market research interview and we are Business & Market Research based in Stockport.'

Market research agencies can subscribe to a service operated by the Market Research Society* which allows them to refer the respondent to a freephone number where the details of the agency can be confirmed.

---

*The Market Research Society, 15 Northburgh Street, London EC1V OAH; 071 490 4911

9

GETTING THE QUESTIONNAIRE RIGHT

■

USING SOFTWARE TO DESIGN AND EDIT QUESTIONNAIRES

The process of arriving at a questionnaire which works, and is as near perfect as possible, comes from constant refining, polishing and editing.

Editing questionnaires has been made easier by word processing which allows words and phrases to be removed or inserted. Questions can be moved around the document. Questions which have been tried and tested can be copied in from other files. Paragraph numbering can be used for question numbers so that they are automatically adjusted if the question order is changed. Spell checking helps remove embarrassing errors. Different font sizes and the use of columns can produce a questionnaire which is almost to desktop publishing standard. Word processing has now become such an important tool in the design of questionnaires that the researcher who cannot type or use the software is at a marked disadvantage.

Special software is also available to assist in questionnaire design. Often this questionnaire design facility is allied to data processing packages such as Snap, Marquis and Merlin.* The

---

*Snap is from Mercator, Bristol; Marquis from Systems Makers, Stockport; Merlin is from Merlinco, London.

packages have value in providing structure to questionnaire design as they remind the researcher to do routine things like give a title, make provision for the respondent's name and address and they provide automatic question numbering and routing. They are especially useful for taking control of the formatting of questions on the page, producing well laid out grids, columns for office use and correctly spaced lines for open-ended responses.

Most of the packages will convert the questionnaires for use in Computer Aided Telephone Interviewing (CATI). CATI is most suitable for large telephone studies where the interviewer reads questions from a computer screen and taps the answers into the keyboard as they are given. Such interviewing works best when the questions and answers are very simple and all the response categories have been pre-empted. The major advantages of CATI interviewing are savings in the time and cost of data processing and analyses of the findings can be obtained at any time during the interview programme.

Questionnaire design packages suffer limitations. Most lack spell checkers. They bring to the screen one question at a time making it difficult to scroll backwards and forwards to look at what has already been asked. For the researcher who is already struggling with the complications of word processing software, the questionnaire design packages are something extra to learn. At least the word processing software is in day-to-day use, finding wider applications in report and letter writing. On balance, therefore, the word processing approach to questionnaire design appears to have more attractions.

It is normal, probably healthy, to produce three or four drafts of the questionnaire before the researcher feels that it is approaching the stage where it is ready for use in the field. Every time a draft is run off, the researcher should be viewing each question critically:

- How will the answer to this question help meet the objectives of the study; is it really necessary?
- Will the question be understood in the way that is intended?
- Is there a better way of asking the question?

■ Is it clear what the interviewer should do and where he or she goes next?

■ Have all the questions been included; has anything been missed out?

PILOTING THE QUESTIONNAIRE

Piloting is where a small number of interviews are carried out in the field to see if there are any aspects of the questionnaire which do not work. First, the researcher should at the very least read it out to him/herself or, better still, ask a colleague to play the role of respondent. Bringing the questionnaire into the *spoken* word could expose weaknesses in wording or phraseology and should show any glaring inconsistencies. It is worth giving a final draft of the questionnaire to the data processing team to see if they can spot any coding or routing problems. The questionnaire can then be passed to the interviewing team for piloting.

Finally, the questionnaire is ready for piloting. The following checks are vital at the pilot stage:

■ Question wording — does it make sense?

■ Pre-codes in closed questions — are they the right ones?

■ Interviewer instructions — is it clear to the interviewer what should be read out and what should not?

■ Routing — does the interviewer know where to go next?

■ Space — is there sufficient space for the answers?

The number of interviews which need to be carried out in the pilot varies according to the type of study. If the full study involves just 50 to 100 interviews with businesses, perhaps half a dozen pilot interviews will be sufficient to see if the questionnaire is working. In fact, in such a small survey, almost every interview will be watched closely and variations and special comments can all be accommodated.

In a larger study, say one involving more than 200 people, the size of the pilot could be between 20 and 50 interviews — sufficient to cover a good cross-section of the respondents.

The pilot should be carried out using the same medium that will be used in the interviews when they finally take place. That is, a telephone interview programme should be piloted over the telephone, street interviews should be piloted in the street. It is important that the person who carries out the pilot is an experienced interviewer, someone who can look out for and pick up weaknesses in the questionnaire if they exist. Given the small number of interviews that will be carried out, the pilot could be undertaken by just one person.

The pilot could be used to build a list of pre-coded answers to an open question although normally these pre-codes would be determined during an earlier, qualitative stage.

The pilot interviews need not be wasted. Very often no changes are required to the questionnaire and so the pilot interviews are perfectly acceptable contributions to the total quota. Even minor changes to the questionnaire need not be a barrier to including the pilot interviews within the total number that are to be carried out, especially if respondents can be recontacted to ask a supplementary question or check if a change of wording would have altered their answer.

In some industrial samples it is not possible to abandon the pilot interviews, as to do so would be to get rid of essential contributors to the survey. It makes sense for companies selected for the pilot interviews in an industrial study to be relatively minor players, thus minimising any damage to the whole survey if they need to be forsaken.

10

SPECIAL QUESTIONNAIRES

◼

The bulk of this book has been devoted to designing structured and semi-structured questionnaires of a type which find application in telephone or face-to-face situations and where there are dozens, probably hundreds of respondents. In this chapter we turn to two contrasting types of questionnaire. One is the checklist which is employed in the more loosely structured work of the qualitative researcher, the other is the self-completion questionnaire which is a very tightly structured form used in postal surveys.

CHECKLISTS

Qualitative researchers work with small samples of respondents and do not attempt to interview masses of people in order to arrive at measurements of how many said one thing and how many said the other. Their interest is in explaining why and how things happen and understanding buyers' motivations. The qualitative researcher works in a more unstructured fashion, interviewing small numbers of people in group discussions* or in

---

*Group discussions (or focus groups) are a research technique used to find out about people's attitudes. They are particularly appropriate for testing new products or concepts. A group comprises 6 to 8 people specially recruited, perhaps because they are a target for the product. The group is led by a researcher (sometimes referred to as a moderator) who uses a checklist to guide the discussion. The group generates ideas and sparks thoughts which would not arise in one-to-one interviewing.

one-to-one depth interviews. The wide ranging responses which are obtained may be recorded on tape or in note form on a pad and some considerable skill and experience is required to interpret and diagnose the findings.

In many respects the checklist (sometimes called a topic list) used by the qualitative researcher is much easier to design than the structured questionnaire. It is really an *aide mémoire*, and the chances are that the researcher who designs it is the same person who will use it. In these conditions, the questions are already in the researcher's head and the checklist is simply a reminder to jog the memory or to tick off the points which have been covered.

There are no hard and fast rules for the design of checklists. Some researchers do not couch the questions in a form ready for asking and they are just listed as subjects. Some have lengthy lists with reminders as to the lines of questioning which will result from certain answers; others simply list a few points to raise in discussion. The following checklist was used to guide discussion groups of householders to find out if they had any views on the environmental aspects of milk carton packaging. In this example the researcher placed a note on the check list as a reminder about the time to be spent on each subject area.

CARTON PACKAGING

1   INTRODUCTION (5 mins)
1.1   Who we are. What we do. What we will be doing tonight.
1.2   Introductions all round.

2   TALK ABOUT MILK PACKAGING (10 mins)
2.1   How many different types of milk packaging can people think of? PROBE: glass, plastic, cartons, sachets.
2.2   What are the advantages/plus points of each? Why? (*Note any mention of environmental issues for later discussion*).
2.3   What are the disadvantages/minus points of each? Why? (*Note any mention of environmental issues for later discussion*).

3   TALK ABOUT PACKAGING MATERIALS IN GENERAL (10 mins)

3.1   What are the advantages of glass, tin, paper, card, plastic as packaging materials?

3.2   What are the disadvantages of glass, tin, paper, card, plastic as packaging materials?

3.3   Which are most environmentally friendly? Why?

3.4   Which are least environmentally friendly? Why?

3.5   Which types of packaging materials are avoided if there is a choice? Why?

4   TALK ABOUT CARTON PACKAGING IN GENERAL (10 mins)

4.1   What products are packed in cartons nowadays?

4.2   What are the good points about carton packaging?

4.3   What are the bad points about carton packaging?

4.4   Do people actively seek cartons in preference to other types of packaging?

4.5   Do people avoid buying products in cartons, preferring other types of packaging?

4.6   Could more products be sold in cartons? **PROBE:** doorstep milk, bottled water, sauces, soups, beans, pet food, flour. What would be the advantages? What would be the disadvantages?

4.7   Which manufacturers of carton packaging are known?

5   NOW TALK ABOUT GLASS AS A PACKAGING MATERIAL (10 mins)

5.1   Is glass environmentally friendly/unfriendly?

5.2   What are the environmental problems of using glass — both in production, in use, and in recycling?

6   TALK ABOUT CHEMICALS USED IN PACKAGING MATERIALS MANUFACTURING (10 mins)

6.1   Is there anything about the *manufacturing process* of *any* packaging material that is environmentally unfriendly? What is it?

6.2   Why is it unfriendly? What are the implications to the user? What are the implications to the environment?

7 TALK ABOUT DIOXIN (10 mins)

7.1 What are the most unfriendly chemicals used in packaging manufacture? What type of packaging are they used in? Why are they unfriendly?

7.2 What is known of .... as a chemical used in the manufacture of packaging materials?

7.3 What is known of .... as a chemical used in the manufacture of packaging materials?

7.4 What is known of dioxin as a chemical used in the manufacture of packaging materials?

7.5 Which types of companies use dioxin? How is it used? What does it do to the packaging? What does it do to the user? What does it do to the environment?

7.6 What are the alternatives to dioxin? How good or bad are these?

8 DIFFERENT SUBJECT NOW. TALK ABOUT MESSAGES ON PACKAGING (10 mins)

8.1 What messages should be shown on different types of packaging material. Which types of packaging are they likely to be on?

Nearly always the qualitative researcher would expect to formulate the specific questions themselves during the interview or group discussion and not worry too much about the precision that is the concern of the quantitative researcher. The qualitative researcher is allowed this freedom being the person who administers the question, hears the answer, develops the discussion with a rejoinder and interprets what it all means.

The qualitative researcher works in the informal atmosphere of conversation and spends much time listening, using silence to flush out further response. Whereas structured interviews last between 15 minutes and up to an hour, the conversational approach used in qualitative research allows the interview length to be pushed well beyond an hour without boredom or weariness on the part of the respondent. The interviews are usually face-to-face and are likely to be held in a home or office (sometimes a special venue is used for group discussions or depth interviews). In certain circumstances, such as with business-to-business research, respondents can be held in discussion for long periods over the telephone as long as the subject is interesting and the interviewer is skilled in building a rapport.

The checklist may appear to play a subservient role in the interview, perhaps being alluded to only now and then, but its importance should not be underestimated. The very act of creating the checklist will help the researcher to structure thoughts and direct the interview.

SELF-COMPLETION AND POSTAL QUESTIONNAIRES

As the name suggests, self-completion questionnaires are those which respondents complete on their own. In the main these are sent through the post and so they are often referred to as postal questionnaires. However, self-completion questionnaires can be used in face-to-face interviews in the right circumstances, perhaps for scalar questions where it is easier for respondents to read the questions and tick the boxes themselves rather than go through the much longer rigmarole of having the interviewer read everything out.

Postal questionnaires are the most difficult of all to design. A poor questionnaire can still be made to work by a skilled and trained interviewing force whereas a questionnaire which has arrived through the post is without anyone to provide advice, answer queries or ensure that the respondent understands the meaning of the questions.

Self-completion questionnaires which are part of face-to-face interviews are rather different as the interviewer is on hand to solve problems.

An example of a postal questionnaire is shown on the following pages. This questionnaire was printed on A3 paper, folded to make four pages, with the first page forming the cover letter.

BUSINESS & MARKET RESEARCH PLC

BUXTON ROAD, HIGH LANE VILLAGE, STOCKPORT, CHESHIRE SK6 8DX
TELEPHONE (0663) 765115 FAX (0663) 762362

Dear Student

As a result of a Bill currently going through the British Parliament, polytechnics in the UK will be redesignated as universities later this year. The consequent change of name, for those of us who are in cities which already contain well established universities, could produce some difficulties. Retaining the name of Manchester in the title is very important because the City has proved such an attraction to students in the past. However, the new name has to make us distinctive from neighbouring sister institutions and several possibilities have been discussed.

This is more than just a name change; it is a re-positioning of Manchester Polytechnic in the field of education. Any change in status will affect you. As part of the consultative process, I would be grateful if you would give the following questions your serious attention. It should not take more than a few minutes of your time as the questionnaire has been designed to be quickly and easily answered.

There are no right or wrong answers to the questions so please just put down what you feel is correct for you.

May I conclude by pointing out that there is no space to record your name and so your reply will be absolutely anonymous. However, we are sampling only a fraction of the people at the Polytechnic and so every questionnaire we hand out we would like returned. We are working to a tight timetable and need your reply by Friday at the latest. Please complete it straight away and place it in one of the boxes close to the entry of your building.

Thank you in anticipation for your help.

Yours sincerely

Paul Hague
Director
29 January 1992

Serial No: Cols (1-4) (5) 1

How to complete this questionnaire

Please write your answer in the space provided or circle the appropriate code. *Ignore the small numbers in brackets which are for data processing and office use only.*

About yourself

This section asks for some details on yourself which will help us classify your answers.

1   Your age on entry to the Poly:

20 or under	1 (6)
21 - 24	2
25 or over	3

2   Your sex:

Male	1 (7)
Female	2

3   Your faculty:

Art & Design	1 (8)
Comm studies & Ed	2
Hollings	3
Human, Law & Soc Sci	4
Mangmt & Business	5
Science & Engineering	6
Other	7

4   Is your course:

Full time	1 (9)
Part time	2

5   The qualification for which you are studying:

HND	1 (10)
Diploma in Higher Education	2
First degree	3
Post graduate/research	4
Professional/other	5

6   Your normal residence before the Poly:

Greater Manchester	1 (11)
Elsewhere in North West	2
Yorkshire & Humberside	3
London & South East	4
West Midlands	5
East Midlands	6
Elsewhere in UK	7
Europe (not UK)	8
Africa	9
Far East	10
Elsewhere in the world	11

7   What year are you in on your current course?

First	1 (12)
Second	2
Third	3
Fourth (or more)	4

Your rating of
Manchester Polytechnic

This section explores your attitudes to Manchester Polytechnic.

8   Which *two* factors had most influence on your coming to Manchester Polytechnic?

First factor   ....   (13 - 15)

Second factor   ....   (16 - 18)

9   Now you are a student at Manchester Polytechnic you may feel able to rate it on various features. Please work through the following list giving Manchester Polytechnic a score out of 5 for each feature. (5 is very good and 1 is very poor). Write your score on the line opposite the feature. If you feel you cannot rate the feature, leave it blank.

The courses at Manchester Polytechnic

Content of the courses	_____	(19)
Promotion of the courses	_____	(20)

Location

Manchester as an enjoyable place	_____	(21)
Manchester as a cultural place	_____	(22)
Friendliness of Manchester people	_____	(23)

The facilities of Manchester Polytechnic

The buildings	_____	(24)
Libraries	_____	(25)
Students' Union	_____	(26)
Dining facilities	_____	(27)
Halls of residence	_____	(28)
Computing facilities	_____	(29)
Other equipment	_____	(30)
Sports facilities	_____	(31)

The teaching staff at Manchester Polytechnic

Teaching skills	_____	(32)
Practical experience	_____	(33)
Academic qualifications	_____	(34)
Caring attitude	_____	(35)

Academic standards of Manchester Polytechnic

Reputation amongst employers	_____	(36)
Reputation amongst friends	_____	(37)

Social life at Manchester Polytechnic

Friendliness	_____	(38)
Clubs and societies	_____	(39)
Student's social life	_____	(40)

Career advantage of Manchester Polytechnic

Long term relevance to career	_____	(41)

Your preferences for other polytechnics or universities

This question is to find out the polytechnics and universities which were in competition with Manchester Polytechnic.

10   Thinking about all the places you really wanted to study, *irrespective of whether they offered you a place or not*, was Manchester Polytechnic your:

First choice	1 (42)
Second choice	2
Third or lower choice	3

11   On the dotted lines below, please list two other colleges, polytechnics or universities, which were your preferred alternatives if you had not come to Manchester Polytechnic.

First alternative   .... (43 - 50)

Second alternative   .... (51 - 57)

Repeat cols (1 - 4) Col (5) 2

Your rating of a new name

This final question is to determine your preference for a new name for Manchester Polytechnic.

12   Please consider a number of new names which have been proposed for Manchester Polytechnic and give each a score out of 5 (5 is high, 1 is low) for your views on its "student appeal", its "quality image", and its "appropriateness". In taking into consideration the name, please also consider the initials and colloquialism by which you think the institution will eventually be known.

	Student Appeal	Quality Image	Appropriateness
All Saints University Of Manchester (ASUM)	_____ (6)	_____ (17)	_____ (28)
City of Manchester University (CMU)	_____ (7)	_____ (18)	_____ (29)
Greater Manchester University (GMU)	_____ (8)	_____ (19)	_____ (30)
John Dalton University of Manchester (JDUM)	_____ (9)	_____ (20)	_____ (31)
Manchester All Saints University (MASU)	_____ (10)	_____ (21)	_____ (32)
Manchester City University (MCU)	_____ (11)	_____ (22)	_____ (33)
Manchester Grosvenor University (MGU)	_____ (12)	_____ (23)	_____ (34)
Manchester John Dalton University (MJDU)	_____ (13)	_____ (24)	_____ (35)
Manchester Metropolitan University (MMU)	_____ (14)	_____ (25)	_____ (36)
Manchester Polytechnic (ie same name)	_____ (15)	_____ (26)	_____ (37)
Manchester Queens/Queen Elizabeth University (MQU)	_____ (16)	_____ (27)	_____ (38)

13   If you would like to suggest an alternative name for Manchester Polytechnic, please do so on the dotted line below.

.... (39 - 49)

Post your questionnaire in the ballot box at the entrance to a main building by Friday, the 31st January.

In postal surveys the response rate is critical. There are various factors which affect response rates:

THE INTEREST FACTOR

The factor that influences the response rate of a postal question-naire, more than anything else, is the interest that the respondent has in the subject of the survey. Thus, a postal survey of customers will achieve a higher response than one of non-customers because there is an *interest* in and a *relationship* between customers and the sponsor of the study. A postal survey aimed at people who have just bought a new truck will generate a high response (over 30 per cent and possibly over 50 per cent) because they are *interested* in the vehicle. If the same respondent received a ques-tionnaire asking about the type of pen he uses, the response would be minimal (probably less than five per cent) because the subject is not compelling. This fundamental point means that researchers should avoid using postal surveys except when the respondent is likely to be highly motivated to answer.

Beyond the intrinsic interest which is held in a subject, the researcher can do a number of things to improve response rates to postal surveys. These are discussed below.

THE INCENTIVE

A respondent does not want to feel that his efforts in completing the questionnaire are a waste of time. It is important, therefore, that the cover letter gives the purpose to the study and convinces the recipient that his or her reply really matters. If possible a benefit should be mentioned such as the promise of better products or service or a gift. Sometimes it is appropriate to offer a summary of the findings.

THE LAYOUT

As in all other questionnaires the postal questionnaire must be orderly and logical, but more so. More than in telephone or face-

to-face interviews, there is a need to begin with easy questions —
questions that involve the simple ticking of boxes — and moving
eventually to those requiring more thought. Getting the respondent
started with the first tick is the hardest task of all and difficult
questions at this stage would be off-putting. Ideally, the questionnaire should be desktop published and of a good print quality. A
professionally produced questionnaire will lift the response. (As
always there are exceptions and a questionnaire that looks as if it
was designed specifically for the recipient by knocking it up on
an old typewriter has been known to yield a high response!)

Instructions must be clear. There is no chance of providing any
further explanation as to what is really meant by a question.
There must be adequate room to answer questions — especially
any that attempt to elicit a free response.

THE CONVENIENCE FACTOR

It has been emphasised that the successful postal questionnaire
must be easy to complete. This means that questions with pre-
coded answers should be used wherever possible. All the
respondent should be asked to do is tick a box. In some circumstances questionnaires with numbers to circle are acceptable but
if there is any doubt, defer to simplicity and use boxes.

Everything should be done to make it easy for the respondent
to reply. The enclosure of a stamped addressed envelope, or at
least a business reply envelope, will raise the response by the odd
percentage point.

DESIGNING COVER LETTERS FOR POSTAL QUESTIONNAIRES

The cover letter accompanying the questionnaire is as important
as the questionnaire itself. Unless there is absolute certainty
about the name and position of the respondent, it is better to
address the letter to 'The householder' or, in the case of business-
to-business surveys, a functional title such as 'The Production
Manager' or 'The Office Equipment Buyer'. Mis-spelling a name

or using the name of someone who has long since left the company or address is worse than having no name at all.

Rules for writing good cover letters are as follows:

■ Explain the purpose of the survey and why the respondent has been selected.

■ Give the respondent a reason for wanting to complete the questionnaire — offer a benefit of one kind or another.

■ Give clear instructions as to what should be done — how to fill it in *and* how to send it back.

■ Give an assurance that completing the questionnaire is easy.

■ If it is possible to do so, give an assurance that replies will be confidential.

■ Thank the respondent.

TYPES OF QUESTIONS SUITED TO POSTAL QUESTIONNAIRES

Pre-coded questions are suited to postal questionnaires as they save the respondent time writing in the answers. Scalar questions are highly applicable to self-completion questionnaires because they can be completed quickly by ticking boxes.

The researcher needs to have a good background on a subject to design a workable self completion questionnaire with sensible pre-coded answers. It would not be possible to construct the following question without some previous knowledge of who makes pipe lagging products. (And this question is as complicated as is possible in a self-completion questionnaire).

Which of the companies listed below would you say has the widest range of pipe lagging products? TICK *ONE COMPANY ONLY* IN COLUMN A.

And which company has the smallest range? TICK *ONE COMPANY ONLY* IN COLUMN B.

	Column A **Widest Range**	Column B **Smallest Range**
Jiffy	☐	☐
Climatube	☐	☐
Jetlag	☐	☐
Tublite	☐	☐
Armaflex	☐	☐
Insultube	☐	☐
Don't know	☐	☐

TYPES OF QUESTIONS NOT SUITED TO POSTAL QUESTIONNAIRES

Open-ended questions do not yield a good response in a self-completion questionnaire. Questions which ask for free-ranging explanations get inadequate (and often illegible) answers such as 'because it is good', 'we have always bought it', 'it does its job' etc and there is no opportunity to find out why it is good, why they always buy it or in what way it does its job.

Nor is it possible to ask complicated questions in a self-completion questionnaire. A question which asks a builders' merchant for a detailed breakdown of his purchases of pipe lagging products over the last year will not be answered because the respondent will not have the answer to mind. The researcher stands some chance if a pre-coded answer is given and the respondent only needs to give a response between ranges:

Finally, about how much did your branch spend on all types of pipe lagging in the last complete year?

Under £1,000	☐
£1,000 to £20,000	☐
£20,001 to £50,000	☐
Over £50,000	☐

In a self-completion questionnaire it is not possible to disclose information in a controlled fashion as in a telephone or visit interview because respondents could (and probably will) read ahead and become aware of forthcoming questions. In an administered questionnaire, the name of the sponsor is often disclosed towards the end, sometimes with special questions to find out what is thought of the company. Such unveiling cannot be used in a self-completion questionnaire.

Complicated routing must be avoided in postal surveys. Skipping questions creates confusion and leads to errors in completion.

▮▮

EXAMPLES OF QUESTIONS

▪

In this final chapter a number of sample questions are presented which can be used as templates for constructing a questionnaire.

QUESTIONS FOR STARTING THE QUESTIONNAIRE

In consumer research it is normal to screen out people who should be excluded from the surveys. Very often exclusions are applied to those employed in market research, advertising or those involved in some way with the study itself. Thus, in a survey which tested the advertising awareness of heating appliances, it was thought necessary to screen out people who work for one of the gas or electric utilities. The screens eliminate people who are not relevant to the detailed questioning which follows later. Note that in the sample question below, no mention is made of the theme of advertising at the time of introducing the interview because the researcher may wish to creep up on the subject.

Q1　Good morning/afternoon. I'm from Business & Market Research. We are carrying out a survey about energy usage and would be grateful if you could spare some time to answer a few questions. The interview will take around 20 minutes.

Firstly, can I check whether you or any members of your household work in any of the following occupations? **READ OUT.**

Journalism/the Media	1 }
Marketing/market research	2 } **CLOSE**
Advertising	3 }
British Gas/An electricity company	4 }
None of these	5 — **CONTINUE**

Q2 And what is your main ITV station? **READ OUT IF NECESSARY.**

Granada	1 } **CONTINUE**
Border	2 }
Other	3 — **CLOSE**

If the first question in the questionnaire is not there to screen people, it could act to win people's interest or to get them talking. In a business-to-business interview it can be helpful to ask a question which enables the interviewer understand all the responses which will follow. The opening question could be almost a 'how are you' in a business capacity.

Q1 My questions are all about adhesives but just before I start, would you tell me what you make at your factory? It will help my understanding of your answers to other questions.

_____

_____

The researcher may need some product knowledge from the outset and we have seen in an earlier question about the Prelude (Chapter 7) how this can be collected.

Equally, at an early juncture, it may be important to find out the part that the respondent plays in the buying decision:

Q   Can I start by asking you which of these statements best
describes your involvement in choosing your suppliers
of electric motors?

I usually make the decision alone   1 → *proceed*

I have most influence but as part of a team
  or group   2 → *proceed*

I have some influence as part of a team or
  group   3 → *proceed*
                                                      but ask:

What influence? Who are the others who are involved in the
decision?

_____

_____

QUESTIONS FOR TESTING THE AWARENESS OF BRANDS OR COMPANIES

Researchers very often want to test the awareness of brands or
companies. This is usually achieved in two stages, first asking the
question without prompting and then using a prompted list. The
names which are given in the unprompted questioning may be
left out of the prompted question but coded up by the interviewer.
The subject of study in the sample question which follows (see
below) was a special type of printing press. The interview was
administered over the telephone and the interviewers were
allowed to script their own introductions following a number of
guidelines. As it happens, the awareness question was also the
first question in the questionnaire and acted to move the
respondents' minds into gear and get them thinking about the
manufacturers of the machines.

MAKE CONTACT WITH THE APPROPRIATE RESPONDENT.
EXPLAIN THAT THE SURVEY IS ABOUT ATTITUDES TO MANU-
FACTURERS OF FLEXOGRAPHIC PRINTING PRESSES WITH A
VIEW TO HELPING MANUFACTURERS IMPROVE THEIR PRODUCTS
AND SERVICE. IF ASKED, SAY THAT THE IDENTITY OF THE
SPONSOR WILL BE DISCLOSED AT THE END OF THE INTERVIEW.

**GIVE AN ASSURANCE THAT ALL RESPONSES WILL BE CONFI-
DENTIAL AND ONLY THE POOLED RESULTS WILL BE USED.**

Q1 Can I start by asking you to think about the manufacturers of flexographic printing presses. Which names
come to mind? **DO *NOT* PROMPT.**

Ameriflex/Wolverine	1
Schiavi-Padani	2
Carrint	3
CMF	4
Cobden Chadwick	5
Comexi	6
Fischer & Krecke (F & K)	7
Flexotechnica	8
Kidder-Stacy	9
PCMC	10
Uteco	11
Windmoeller & Hoelscher (W & H)	12
Others _____	
Others _____	

Q2 Now I would like to read out some companies which
make flexographic printing presses. As I read them out
would you tell me which you have heard of? **ROTATE
START. TICK START. CIRCLE THOSE MEN-
TIONED IN Q1 WITHOUT READING THEM OUT.**

Ameriflex/Wolverine	1
Schiavi-Padani	2
Carrint	3
CMF	4
Cobden Chadwick	5
Comexi	6
Fischer & Krecke (F & K)	7
Flexotechnica	8
Kidder-Stacy	9
PCMC	10
Uteco	11
Windmoeller & Hoelscher (W & H)	12

Q3   I am now moving on to talk about how you started dealing with your printing press suppliers. First can I check the makes of printing presses installed at your plant?

Q4   FOR EACH MAKE USED ASK: And what is the application for this manufacturer's machines — is it for paper sacks, linerboard, tissue, wallcoverings etc?

Q3 Make of printing presses installed	Q4 Application of press

A further sophistication to this question could be to record separately the order in which people list the brands. The companies or brands which are mentioned first can be assumed to be more 'front of mind' than those which are mentioned second or third.

Q1   I would like to ask you some questions about petrol. Off the top of your head can you give me the names of some petrol companies? DO NOT PROMPT. RECORD BELOW IN ORDER GIVEN.

	First	Second	Third
		Mentioned	
BP	1	1	1
Burmah	2	2	2
Elf	3	3	3
Esso	4	4	4
Gulf	5	5	5
Jet/Conoco	6	6	6
Mobil	7	7	7
Shell	8	8	8

| | First | Second | Third |
		Mentioned	
Texaco	9	9	9
Total	10	10	10
Hypermarket (specify)	11	11	11
....			
Other (specify)	12	12	12
....			

QUESTIONS FOR OBTAINING BEHAVIOURAL INFORMATION

In one respect, behavioural questions are the simplest to ask but there can be problems deciding on sensible intervals for a fixed response. With some questions the subject is within everyday experience and the responses are easy to anticipate. The following example is about petrol purchasing and some licence has been taken in the intervals which are used for the buying frequency.

Q2 Now thinking about buying petrol or diesel. How often do you buy petrol/diesel? **READ OUT LIST — CIRCLE ONE CODE ONLY.**

Every day	1
2 to 3 times a week	2
Once a week	3
2 to 3 times a month	4
Less often	5

Even where the subject is relatively commonplace, such as buying petrol, the way people behave can be quite complicated. In such circumstances it could be worth thinking about reducing the response categories to phrases with which people can identify.

Q3 Which of the phrases on this card (**SHOW CARD**) best describes how you buy petrol?

Buy most of your petrol from one particular station   1

Buy most of your petrol at 2 or 3 stations and they are
   all the same brand   2

Buy most of your petrol at 2 or 3 stations and they are
   all different brands   3

Buy your petrol at many different stations but usually
   the same brand   4

Buy your petrol at many different stations and
   many different brands   5

Buy most of your petrol at a hypermarket   6

Something other than these (please specify)   7

Researchers often have to work around subjects where they have
no inkling of what the answer could be and in these circumstances open-ended responses are used. The next example comes
from a survey of packaged sewage treatment plant. This sort of
equipment is bought relatively infrequently and so the interval
over which the question relates is two years and this needs to be
emphasised. The terminology used to describe the products may
be alien to the reader of this book but it was common parlance to
respondents in the industry. A grid type question was used to
reduce the space taken up on the page.

Q3a   Would you tell me how many *trickling filtration* plants
        your establishment has installed in the last *two*
        years? **REPEAT FOR ROTATING BIOLOGICAL,
        CONTACT STABILISATION AND 'OTHERS'.**

Q3b   How many of these plants are for stand alone situa-
        tions?

Q3c   How many are extensions to existing plants?

Type of plant	**3a** **Number** **installed** **over 2 yrs**	**3b** **Stand** **alone**	**3c** **Extensions** **to plants**
Trickling filtration	_____	_____	_____
Rotating biological	_____	_____	_____
Contact stabilisation	_____	_____	_____
Others (specify)	_____	_____	_____

QUESTIONS FOR OBTAINING ATTITUDINAL INFORMATION

A very common approach to asking attitudes to products is to ask the simple question *why?*

Q   Why did you not consider an electric central heating system?

_____

_____

_____

So scalar questions are frequently used to obtain attitudinal information. The 'how likely' scale must be one of the most popular.

Q   How likely are you to consider buying .... in the next year?

Very likely	1
Quite likely	2
Neither likely nor unlikely	3
Quite unlikely	4
Very unlikely	5

Those who answered codes 3, 4 or 5 would probably be asked '*why?*'.

Attitudes people have to a product can be obtained by asking them to agree or disagree with statements. In order to avoid the respondent getting into a groove and giving the same answer consistently, the positive and negative statements can be mixed up, as in the following example. Also, there is no opportunity for sitting on the fence: people have to say whether they either agree or disagree with the statements.

Q   Having used the toothpaste, would you now tell me if you agree or disagree with the following statements. Choose one of the levels of agreement off this card to tell me what you think. SHOW CARD. READ OUT EACH STATEMENT IN TURN. ROTATE START. TICK START.

	Agree Strongly	Agree Slightly	Disagree Slightly	Disagree Strongly
Tastes very minty	1	2	3	4
Feels gritty	1	2	3	4
Tastes sweet	1	2	3	4
Hasn't got much taste	1	2	3	4
Makes my mouth feel fresh	1	2	3	4
Feels smooth	1	2	3	4

QUESTIONS FOR FINDING OUT ABOUT BUYING MOTIVATIONS

Surveys frequently need to find out why people buy in a certain way. The obvious and direct question can often be the best.

Q1   What above all else influences the choice of your supplier of ....?

_____

_____

_____

This type of open-ended questioning could be extended to include specific probes on the significance of subjects of interest such as the importance of price, quality, delivery, technical service and so on. Some of these issues are subjects in their own right. For example, price could be opened up to include net price paid, credit terms and rebates. Delivery covers availability off the shelf, delivery on time. Quality includes durability, reliability and integrity.

Beyond the open-ended questioning, the researcher could consider prompted questions to explore buying motivations. One approach to this could be where the respondent is asked to 'trade off' the various factors in the buying decision by spending points out of 10.

Of course, the previous question presupposes that some preliminary work has been carried out to show which are the important factors people are interested in trading off.

The example below has a list which is read out and pushes the limits of people's memories. Most respondents can cope with the question but, in an ideal world, the list would have been half the length.

Q   I will now read out a list of factors which some people have said are important in influencing their choice of

Factor	Points out of 10
Delivery just in time	
Reliable delivery	
The lowest price	
Reliable motors	
Motor is specified by customer	
Supplies non-standard designs	
Noise level	
Made to IEC standard	
Can supply electronic controls	
Service/back up facilities	
Other (specify _____)	
T O T A L (must add to 10)	10

suppliers of electric motors. To measure how important you think they are I would like you to allocate 10 points across the different factors. The more important a factor, the more points you should give it. But the more points you give to one factor, the less there are to give to the others. First I will read out the list. READ LIST. ROTATE ORDER. TICK START. TOTAL MUST ADD TO 10. Now, how would you like to spend your 10 points?

QUESTIONS FOR TESTING CUSTOMERS' PREFERENCES FOR DIFFERENT PRODUCTS

This book emphasises the benefits of keeping questions and questionnaires as simple as possible. Over-complicated questions lead to problems for the field force, for the analysis team and for the person who has to make sense of them when the work is completed. However, there are occasions when simple questions are not good enough. Take for example, questions which seek to find out why people choose certain types of cars. Simple questioning is likely to indicate that safety is one of the most important factors in people's minds and yet evidence of how people act in the car showroom indicates that what people say is not what they do. Researchers have tried to overcome the problem of looking at factors in isolation by grouping them into concepts, the sort that may be relevant to real life situations. Using special computer programmes this data produces an indirect measure of customer preferences and is known as *conjoint analysis*.

Take a simple product such as an envelope which has three different attributes each with two variations.

Method of sealing	Address facility	Colour
Self seal	Window	White
Glue	No window	Brown

It is possible to devise eight different types of envelope concepts from these variations, namely:

Concept	Method of sealing	Address facility	Colour
1	Self seal	Window	White
2	Self seal	Window	Brown
3	Self seal	No window	White
4	Self seal	No window	Brown
5	Glue	Window	White
6	Glue	Window	Brown
7	Glue	No window	White
8	Glue	No window	Brown

Each of these concepts could be presented to a respondent who would be asked to classify them into piles, correspondent to 'very interesting' through to 'not particularly interesting'. Having done this, the respondent is then asked to rank the concepts in each pile to show which is most appealing and least appealing. This type of questioning can work with products which have a relatively small number of concepts but it becomes extremely tedious for the respondent if there are many attributes and therefore many concepts. Twenty five to thirty concepts is about the maximum that should be attempted.

Q   I would like you to look through these cards on which you will see different styles of envelope. Place the cards into three piles which illustrate whether you think that for your company the envelopes would be:

Interesting
Maybe interesting
Not interesting at all.

Now please take each pile in turn and sort them into an order so that the card on the top is the envelope style you think is best for your company and that on the bottom is the one you think is worst.

QUESTIONS FOR TESTING CUSTOMERS' SATISFACTION

Customer satisfaction studies are made up of special types of attitudinal questions which provide benchmarks for comparison with other companies and against which the performance of a company can be judged at some future date if the study is ever repeated. The example shown below is for a special type of printing machine but the format of questions could apply to most products. The questions begin by finding out, in open-ended fashion, what influences the buying decision. This is followed by a prompted question on the same subject. Answers to these questions enable the researchers to show the importance which should be attached to answers to the rating questions. For example, if 'printing quality' proves to be a far more important influence on the buying decision than, say, 'change over time', then 'printing quality' should be the factor which has more of the company's resources devoted to getting it right.

Q1   Can I ask you to imagine that a manufacturer of flexographic printing machines — a name that is known to you — is seeking to win business which you are due to place. What are the factors you would weigh up in deciding whether or not to give them your business?

_____

_____

_____

Q2   I would now like you to think about the importance of some factors which could play a part in the buying decision and help me assemble them in the order of importance from your point of view. I will read the factors out and then would you tell me which is most important, which is second most important, and I will finish with which you think is third most important. **ROTATE ORDER OF START. TICK START. READ LIST.**

Factors Influencing The Buying Decision	RANK
Reputation of the company	
Printing quality	
The change-over time	
The price	
The reliability of the machine	
Delivery	
The availability of automation features	
Other (specify)	

Q3　And now I would like you to tell me what you think of five manufacturers of printing machines, whether or not you use them. I would like you to give me a score out of 5 where 5 is very good and 1 is very poor. (SCORE 6 FOR DON'T KNOW, WON'T SAY) Can I start with ....? (ROTATE ORDER OF COMPANIES) What do you think of it for 'Reputation'? (ROTATE ORDER OF START) (TICK START)

Factors Influencing The Buying Decision	Cobden Chadwick	Fischer & Krecke	Windmoeller & Hoelscher
Reputation of the company			
Printing quality			
Change-over time			
Price			
Reliability of the machines			
Delivery			
Availability of automation features			

Q4 **FOR ANY COMPANY WITH ANY SCORES WHICH ARE 3 OR BELOW ASK:** I see that you gave .... (**NAME COMPANY**) a low score for .... (**NAME ASPECT**) Why was this?

_____

_____

_____

I will now read out some phrases and would like you to tell me to what extent you agree or disagree that they describe three European flexographic press manufacturers. **ROTATE ORDER OF START OF COMPANIES.** A score of 5 means you strongly agree, and a score of 1 means that you strongly disagree.

Statements	Cobden Chadwick	Fischer & Krecke	Windmoeller & Hoelscher
Q5 The company is innovative			
Q6 The company is safe to deal with			
Q7 The company reacts quickly to your requirements			
Q8 The company's product range suits my business			
Q9 The company is pleasant to deal with			
Q10 The company communicates well with its customers			
Q11 The company is very visible in the market			

Here are 8 key questions which could be considered in almost any customer satisfaction survey. In such questioning, any neutral or negative response would be followed by the question, 'Why did you say that?'

Q1   How satisfied are you with the quality of products from ABC Ltd? Are you:

Very satisfied	1
Quite satisfied	2
Neither satisfied nor dissatisfied	3
Not very satisfied	4
Not at all satisfied	5

Q2   How satisfied are you with the reliability of the products from ABC Ltd? Are you:

Very satisfied	1
Quite satisfied	2
Neither satisfied nor dissatisfied	3
Not very satisfied	4
Not at all satisfied	5

Q3   How satisfied are you with the value for money of products from ABC Ltd? Are you:

Very satisfied   1
Quite satisfied   2
Neither satisfied nor dissatisfied   3
Not very satisfied   4
Not at all satisfied   5

Q4   How satisfied are you with the sales service from ABC
     Ltd? Are you:

Very satisfied   1
Quite satisfied   2
Neither satisfied nor dissatisfied   3
Not very satisfied   4
Not at all satisfied   5

Q5   How satisfied are you with the speed of delivery from
     ABC Ltd? Are you:

Very satisfied   1
Quite satisfied   2
Neither satisfied nor dissatisfied   3
Not very satisfied   4
Not at all satisfied   5

Q6   How satisfied are you with the reliability of delivery
     from ABC Ltd? Are you:

Very satisfied   1
Quite satisfied   2
Neither satisfied nor dissatisfied   3
Not very satisfied   4
Not at all satisfied   5

Q7   How likely or unlikely are you to buy from ABC Ltd
     next time you require these products? Would you say
     you are:

Very likely   1
Quite likely   2
Neither likely nor unlikely   3
Not very likely   4
Not at all likely   5

Q8   If you were asked by a friend to suggest a supplier of these products, how likely or unlikely would you be to recommend ABC Ltd? Would you say you were:

Very likely	1
Quite likely	2
Neither likely nor unlikely	3
Not very likely	4
Not at all likely	5

QUESTIONS FOR TESTING THE PRICE PEOPLE WILL PAY FOR A PRODUCT

The price which people are prepared to pay for existing products and services can be ascertained by behavioural and attitudinal questions. There will be occasions when buyers in industry refuse to answer these questions as the information could be commercially sensitive. Do not expect to be able to phone buyers at large superstores and pop a simple question which will tell you how much they are paying for the products within their responsibility. Buyers in the motor industry are similarly circumspect about what they are paying for their components from certain suppliers. In the main, however, buyers in industry and consumers in the home will tell you what they are paying for products and services.

Unless it is essential that the information is precise, it can help to band the responses so that the respondent does not feel obliged to remember the exact money value. The choice of words in the question can sometimes help soften its intrusive nature. In the following question the intervals were chosen to straddle the price points around the £3.50, £4.00, £4.50 etc.

Q   I am trying to obtain an indication of the price of photocopying paper. I shall read out some price bands and I would like you to tell me which band reflects the price your company is paying?

Less than £3.25 per ream	1
£3.26 to £3.75 per ream	2

£3.76 to £4.25 per ream	3
£4.26 to £4.75 per ream	4
£4.76 to £5.25 per ream	5
£5.26 to £5.75 per ream	6
£Over 5.75 per ream (specify)	7
....	
Don't know	8
Refused	9

The researcher may want to plot a demand curve for a product so that the optimum price level for a product can be determined. The following example shows how Regional Railways used a simple test for their customers in which they were asked how likely they would be to make a journey at different price levels. The increases ranged from +3 per cent to +20 per cent and were labelled on a card with letters 'P' to 'T'. These letters 'P' through to 'T' were written in random order on the questionnaire with the corresponding prices against them. Prices were then read to respondents in the order they had been written on the questionnaire (ie random). After each question respondents were asked to state, using a scale, their likelihood of purchasing at that price. The principle of testing prices in random order is an essential part of this type of research. If the prices were to be tested in ascending order (in this case up to +20 per cent), the respondent could be expected to vary the response with each step up the scale rather than considering each absolute price level. This problem is reduced or removed by presenting the prices in random order.

Q   I am now going to read out a number of prices which you might be charged for your ticket for the journey you are making. I would like you to tell me how likely you would be to buy a ticket at each price. **ASK FOR EACH PRICE IN TURN IN THE ORDER RECORDED ON THE QUESTIONNAIRE.**

How likely would you be to buy your ticket at £x? Would you be . . .
Definitely
Very likely

Quite likely
Not very likely
Not at all likely
to buy your ticket at this price?

	P	R	T	U	Q	S
	£..	£..	£..	£..	£..	£..
Definitely	1	1	1	1	1	1
Very likely	2	2	2	2	2	2
Quite likely	3	3	3	3	3	3
Not very likely	4	4	4	4	4	4
Not at all likely	5	5	5	5	5	5
Don't know	6	6	6	6	6	6

This simple method of finding out the optimum price could just as readily be applied to any other product as to a railway ticket. However, the researcher sometimes wants to find out how much people will pay for individual aspects of a product. This information can be useful when deciding on the specification of a new product as it gives the designers some indication of what they could leave out or build in to create a product at the ideal price. One option is to use the *Simalto* technique in which respondents are asked to say which features they would like in an ideal product and then to trade off each of the features by saying whether or not they would buy the product if the feature had a certain price tag. An example of a Simalto questionnaire which was used to test the price of features of a franking machine is given opposite. In the question, the actual details of each respondent's franking machine (called also a mailing machine) were written in the blank boxes. Questioning then determined whether people wanted bigger, better or faster features. Those that did were then asked, in a separate question not shown here, how much more they would pay for the improved features.

QUESTIONS FOR CLASSIFYING RESPONDENTS

Classification questions for consumers could include the following demographic breakdowns:

MID-RANGE MAILING MACHINE

FEATURE	CURRENT	ALTERNATIVE OPTIONS				

Feature	Current	Alternative Options				
Size - height		Bigger	As now	Smaller by 10%	Smaller by 25%	Smaller by 33%
Size - width		Bigger	As now	Smaller by 10%	Smaller by 25%	Smaller by 33%
Size - depth		Bigger	As now	Smaller by 10%	Smaller by 25%	Smaller by 33%

Feature	Current	Alternative Options	
Style		As now	Sleek Desk Top Product

Feature	Current	Alternative Options				
Envelope processing speed		Slower	As now	Faster by 10%	Faster by 25%	Faster by 50%	Faster by 100%

Feature	Current	Alternative Options		
Envelope feed adjustment		Manual adjustment (adjust for thick & thin)	No adjustment required (automatic)	Adjustment for thick & thin (semi-automatic)
Labels		Manual	Automatic single feed	Automatic feed/ keyboard selectable

Feature	Current	Alternative Options			
Envelope stacking		No stacker	25 letters	50 letters	100 letters

Feature	Current	Alternative Options		
Date change		As now	Easier than now	Automatic (clock)
Controls		Wheels	Levers/knobs	Keyboard/display

Feature	Current	Alternative Options			
Noise		As now	Quieter	A lot quieter	Very much quieter
Interface to scale		No interface to scale	Automatic meter setting	Automatic in-line weighing	Scale auto-change B slogan

Q   Thank you for helping me. Just so that we can classify the answers you have given could I ask you a number of short questions about yourself and your household?

Sex (This would not be asked)
Male   1
Female   2

Household status (This classification is now becoming contentious)
Head of household   1
Housewife   2
Other adult   3

Age
17–24   1
25–34   2
35–44   3
45–54   4
55–64   5
65+   6

Marital status
Single   1
Married/partners   2
Widowed   3
Divorced/separated   4

Working status
Full time (30+ hours per week)   1
Part time (8–30 hours per week)   2
Housewife (full time at home)   3
Student (full time)   4
Temporary unemployed   5
Permanently unemployed (eg chronically sick)   6
Retired   7

Socio-economic Grade (SEG)
AB (Managerial)   1
C1 (Supervisory/junior admin)   2
C2 (Skilled manual workers)   3
DE (Semi/unskilled and pensioners) 4

Other consumer classification questions can be used and there are no rigid rules as to what categories to use. If there are government statistics which relate to the subjects, it makes sense to use breaks which are compatible. Examples of categories include:

- income of the head of the household or the respondent;
- final educational level of head of the household or the respondent;
- aggregate income of the household
- type of housing — eg terraced, semi-detached, detached, flats;
- size of house — eg number of bedrooms;
- age of housing;
- location — this could be by government Standard Region, television region or Nielsen regions;
- type of area — eg as indicated by one of the companies which classify neighbourhoods such as Acorn or Pinpoint;
- number of people in the household;
- number of children in the household;
- number of cars in the household; or
- ownership of certain products such as computers or TVs.

In exactly the same way, questions would be asked of business-to-business respondents. There are no fixed categories in these types of surveys and a choice should be made that is useful to the objectives of the study. The following are by way of example and the response categories which are used should be adjusted to suit.

Q   Thank you for helping me. Just so that we can classify the information you have given, could I ask you a number of short questions about the establishment on whose behalf you have been answering?

How many people do you employ at your establishment including both staff and works? **PROMPT WITH RANGES.**

Less than 25	1
25–50	2
51–150	3
151–250	4
251–750	5
Over 750	6

And what is the approximate turnover of your establishment? **PROMPT WITH RANGES.**

Less than £½ million	1
£½ to £¾ million	2
>£¾ to £1½ million	3
>£1½ to £3 million	4
>£3 to £7 million	5
>£7 to £15 million	6
Over £15 million (specify)	7

....

What is the nature of the business carried out at your establishment?

CLASSIFY INTO ONE OF THE FOLLOWING CATEGORIES

Manufacturing	1
Distribution	2
Retailing	3
Services	4
Utilities (gas/water/electricity)	5
Education	6
Government/public service	7
Agriculture/mining/quarrying	8
Other	9

Other classification questions which could be considered for business-to-business surveys are:

■ geographical region — standard region or simply North, Midlands and South;
■ size of spend on a certain product;
■ number of establishments within the group;
■ whether head office or subsidiary.

ROUNDING OFF THE INTERVIEW

In interviews with consumers it is normal practice at the end of the interview to ask for their name and address in order that participants (usually 10 per cent) can be contacted to check that the work was done properly. Whether the respondent is a private consumer or representing a business it is a common courtesy to thank them for the time spent in completing the questions. The interviewer can be left to offer her/his own thanks or they can be scripted onto the questionnaire. In the following example reference is made to a free phone number, available via the Market Research Society, for validating that the company carrying out the research is one which is listed in its directory which lists market research organisations.

> Thank you for your help. Can I just remind you that we are Business & Market Research and that if you want to verify that we are a bonafide market research agency, I can give you the phone number of the Market Research Society to ring. **GIVE FREE PHONE NUMBER IF REQUIRED.**

Alternatively, a simple conclusion could be:

> Thank you for your time in helping me with these questions which I am sure will be useful in helping improve the products and services which you may buy. Can I assure you once again that the information you have given will be treated as absolutely confidential and will only be used as part of a pooled analysis.

BIBLIOGRAPHY

∎

GENERAL READING ON INDUSTRIAL MARKET RESEARCH

Hague, Paul N & Peter Jackson (1987) *Do Your Own Market Research*, Kogan Page, London.

Hague, Paul N & Peter Jackson (1992) *Marketing Research in Practice*, Kogan Page, London.

Hague, Paul N & Peter Jackson (1990) *How To Do Marketing Research*, Kogan Page, London.

MacLean, Ian, ed., (1976) *Handbook of Industrial Marketing Research*, Kluwer-Harrap, Brentford.

Stacey, NAH & Aubrey Wilson (1963) *Industrial Market Research – Management Techniques*, Hutchinson, London.

Sutherland, Ken, ed., (1991) *Researching Business Markets*, Kogan Page on behalf of the Industrial Marketing Research Association, London.

Wilson, Aubrey (1968) *The Assessment of Industrial Markets*, Hutchinson, London.

GENERAL READING ON MARKET RESEARCH (CONSUMER RESEARCH ORIENTATED)

Aaker, David A & George S Day (1990) *Marketing Research,* John Wiley & Sons, Chichester.

Baker, Michael J (1991) *Research For Marketing*, Macmillan, London.

Birn, Robin (1991) *The Effective Use of Market Research*, Kogan Page, London.

Birn R, Hague P & Vangelder P, eds, (1990) *A Handbook of Market Research Techniques*, Kogan Page, London.

Cannon, Tom (1973) *Advertising Research*, Intertext, Aylesbury.

Chisnall, Peter (1992) *Marketing Research*, McGraw-Hill, Maidenhead.

Chisnall, Peter (1991) *The Essence of Marketing Research*, Prentice Hall, Englewood Cliffs, New Jersey.

Crimp, Margaret (1990) *The Marketing Research Process*, Prentice-Hall, Englewood Cliffs, New Jersey.

Crouch, S (1984) *Marketing Research For Managers*, Heinemann, Oxford.

Ehrenberg, ASC (1988) *Repeat Buying*, Edward Arnold, Sevenoaks.

Gordon, Wendy & Roy Langmaid (1988) *Qualitative Market Research*, Gower, Aldershot.

Gorton, Keith & Isobel Doole (1989) *Low-Cost Marketing Research*, John Wiley & Sons, Chichester.

Green, P & J Tull (1978) *Research For Marketing Decisions*, Prentice-Hall, Englewood Cliffs, New Jersey.

Jain AK, P Pinson & B Ratchford (1982) *Marketing Research – Applications and Problems*, John Wiley & Sons, Chichester.

Kreuger, Richard A (1989) *Focus Groups (A Practical Guide For Small Businesses)*, Sage Publications, London.

Robson, S & A Foster, eds, (1989) *Qualitative Research In Action*, Edward Arnold, Sevenoaks.

Talmage, PA (1988) *Dictionary of Marketing Research*, Market Research Society, London.

Walker, R, ed., (1985) *Applied Qualitative Research*, Gower, Aldershot.

Williams, Keith (1981) *Behavioural Aspects of Marketing*, Heinemann, Oxford.

Worcester, RM & J Downam, eds, (1986) *Consumer Market Research Handbook*, Elsevier, Netherlands.

QUESTIONNAIRES

Oppenheim, AN (1970) *Questionnaire Design And Attidue Measurement*, Heinemann, Oxford.

Wolfe, A (1984) *Standardised Questions*, Market Research Society, London.

PRESENTATIONS AND REPORT WRITING

Jay, Anthony (1976) *Slide Rules*, Video Arts, London.

May, John (1982) *How To Make Effective Business Presentations*, McGraw-Hill, London.

STATISTICS

Alt, Mick (1990) *Exploring Hyperspace: A Non-mathematical Explanation of Multivariate Analysis*, McGraw Hill, London.

Gilchrist, Warren (1984) *Statistical Forecasting*, John Wiley & Sons, Chichester.

Moroney, MJ (1953) *Facts From Figures*, Pelican, London.

INDEX

■

LRC Stoke Park
GUILDFORD COLLEGE

GUILDFORD **college**　　7 DAY
BOOK

Learning Resource Centre

Please return on or before the last date shown.
No further issues or renewals if any items are overdue.

- 9 FEB 2010　　1 7 MAR 2011
　　1 1 MAR 2010　2 2 FEB 2012
　3 1 MAR 2010
　- 6 MAY 2010　　2 4 JAN 2013
1 7 MAY 2010

1 7 JUN 2010　　2 5 MAR 2013
1 0 NOV 2010

　　　　1 6 SEP 2013

　　　　2 5 JAN 2017

2 4 JAN 2011
　- 2 MAR 2011

Class: _001.4 HAG_

Title: _QUESTIONNAIRE DESIGN_

Author: _HAGUE, PAUL._

157754